ROUTLEDGE LIBRARY EDITIONS: LIBRARY AND INFORMATION SCIENCE

Volume 25

CREATIVE PLANNING OF SPECIAL LIBRARY FACILITIES

CREATIVE PLANNING OF SPECIAL LIBRARY FACILITIES

Edited by
ELLIS MOUNT

LONDON AND NEW YORK

First published in 1988 by The Haworth Press, Inc.

This edition first published in 2020
by Routledge
2 Park Square, Milton Park, Abingdon, Oxon OX14 4RN

and by Routledge
52 Vanderbilt Avenue, New York, NY 10017

Routledge is an imprint of the Taylor & Francis Group, an informa business

© 1988 The Haworth Press, Inc.

All rights reserved. No part of this book may be reprinted or reproduced or utilised in any form or by any electronic, mechanical, or other means, now known or hereafter invented, including photocopying and recording, or in any information storage or retrieval system, without permission in writing from the publishers.

Trademark notice: Product or corporate names may be trademarks or registered trademarks, and are used only for identification and explanation without intent to infringe.

British Library Cataloguing in Publication Data
A catalogue record for this book is available from the British Library

ISBN: 978-0-367-34616-4 (Set)
ISBN: 978-0-429-34352-0 (Set) (ebk)
ISBN: 978-0-367-36305-5 (Volume 25) (hbk)
ISBN: 978-0-367-36307-9 (Volume 25) (pbk)
ISBN: 978-0-429-34519-7 (Volume 25) (ebk)

Publisher's Note
The publisher has gone to great lengths to ensure the quality of this reprint but points out that some imperfections in the original copies may be apparent.

Disclaimer
The publisher has made every effort to trace copyright holders and would welcome correspondence from those they have been unable to trace.

Creative Planning of Special Library Facilities

Ellis Mount
Editor

The Haworth Press
New York • London

Creative Planning of Special Library Facilities is Volume 1 in the Haworth Series in Special Librarianship.

© 1988 by The Haworth Press, Inc. All rights reserved. No part of this work may be reproduced or utilized in any form or by any means, electronic or mechanical, including photocopying, microfilm and recording, or by any information storage and retrieval system, without permission in writing from the publisher. Printed in the United States of America.

The Haworth Press, Inc., 12 West 32 Street, New York, NY 10001
EUROSPAN/Haworth, 3 Henrietta Street, London WC2E 8LU England

Cover design: The research library at the Central Research Division of Pfizer Inc., in Groton, Connecticut features a reading room that overlooks an interior courtyard. Architect: CUH2A, Photographer: Otto Baitz.

Library of Congress Cataloging-in-Publication Data

Creative planning on special library facilities / Ellis Mount, editor.
   p. cm. — (Haworth series on special librarianship, ISSN 0899-3424 ; v. 1)
   Includes bibliographies and index.
   ISBN 0-86656-697-X. ISBN 0-86656-804-2 (pbk.)
   1. Library planning. 2. Libraries, Special. I. Mount, Ellis. II. Series.
Z679.5.C74 1988
022'3—dc19

88-24633
CIP

CONTENTS

Preface   1

PART I: BASICS OF PLANNING FACILITIES
    Ellis Mount

Chapter 1: An Overview of Library Planning   3

Chapter 2: Preparing the Library Program   9

Chapter 3: Space Utilization   15

Chapter 4: Selection of Equipment and Furnishings   29

Chapter 5: Moving the Library   35

PART II: ADVANCED ASPECTS OF PLANNING FACILITIES

Chapter 6: Pre-Planning Activities: What to Do Before the Architect Arrives   41
    Deborah S. Panella

Chapter 7: Planning: A Cooperative Effort   53
    Arleen N. Somerville

Chapter 8: The Role of the Architect in Library Planning   67
    Robert R. Thrun

Chapter 9: Estimation of Shelving Needs: Selection of Equipment   81
    Tony Stankus
    Kevin Rosseel

Chapter 10: The Role of the Interior Designer in Library Planning   99
    John C. Mudgett

Chapter 11: Furnishing the Electronic Library   111
    Lorraine Schulte

Chapter 12: An Annotated Bibliography on Planning
    Special Libraries   133
    Beverly S. Gordon

Appendix A: Library Facilities of the Oregon Regional
    Primate Research Center   159
    Isabel G. McDonald

Appendix B: The Upjohn Company Corporate Technical
    Library   165
    Lorraine Schulte

Appendix C: Swarthmore College's Science and Engineering
    Library   179
    Michael J. Durkan
    Emi K. Horikawa

Appendix D: Paul, Weiss, Rifkind, Wharton & Garrison
    Library   189
    Deborah S. Panella

Index   195

Preface

This book is an introductory text for those who have had little or no experience in the process of designing a facility for a special library. It is chiefly concerned with the typically small library facilities found in most special libraries that serve corporations, government agencies, not-for-profit organizations, and professional societies. The book may also help those planning relatively small special subject-oriented libraries located in academic institutions and public libraries, such as a chemistry library in a university or a business department of a public library. It applies both to special libraries and information centers. All subject disciplines — such as the sciences, business, the arts — can be served by the libraries developed as a result of using this book.

Planning facilities for special libraries and information centers offers a splendid opportunity for the planners to be creative in their approach. Top administrators and managers in organizations that sponsor such libraries generally support efforts to introduce creativity in the planning process. Creativity by itself, however, is not enough of a goal for the planner. It must be used in conjunction with common sense. The goal of this book, then, is to show ways in which creativity, coupled with the necessary virtue of sound judgment, can be used to plan facilities for special libraries.

It is hoped readers will find this book to be both stimulating and reliable. It should serve not only librarians planning new facilities but also those involved in remodeling or renovating existing facilities.

Part I, is essentially an introduction to the basic processes and procedures involved in planning library facilities. The remainder of the book consists of chapters written by experienced professionals whose contributions elaborate on the basics found in the first part.

Chapters cover all aspects of planning, ranging from steps to take before serious planning sessions get underway to the process of moving into the facility. In addition, the Appendixes contain descriptions and layouts of four typical libraries, each of which shows the result of careful, creative planning. For those wishing additional information beyond the references listed at the end of chapters, there is an extensive annotated bibliography near the end of the book.

I would like to acknowledge the valuable assistance given me by many of my colleagues and associates. Some wished to remain anonymous, and the others are too numerous to try to list. At any rate, their help has been very gratifying to me.

PART I: BASICS OF PLANNING FACILITIES

Chapter 1

An Overview of Library Planning

Planning a new or a remodeled special library facility can be a very satisfying, exhilarating experience. The creation of a facility that incorporates ideas that a librarian may have wanted to use for years is an exciting event that no one ever forgets. At the same time the experience can be time consuming and frustrating, depending upon circumstances. Most librarians, however, feel that even the hard work and the frustrations are worth it when they view the results of the whole process. The enjoyable aspects outweigh the negative ones.

The skill with which the librarian plans the facility has a great deal to do with how smoothly the process goes. Being well prepared for planning a library, even if the planner does not have much experience, can do a lot toward ensuring a relatively peaceful, often enjoyable, experience. The purpose of this book is to provide the planners of special library facilities with enough information and guidance to help them avoid many well known pitfalls and to enable them to be successful in helping to create a well-designed library. No previous experience is required to understand the topics discussed, although it goes without saying that such experience would be an advantage to the reader.

Special librarians should pay particular attention to the process of planning library facilities because they are likely to be asked to plan a new or remodeled facility sometime during their careers. The main reason for this is that many special librarians are either the only professional librarian in a given organization or the most senior librarian on hand, even if they have not been on the staff a long time.

THE ROLE OF CREATIVITY IN PLANNING

New or remodeled library facilities can be dull or interesting, attractive or ugly, poorly designed or cleverly designed. The difference in many cases depends upon the degree of intelligence and creativity possessed by those involved in the planning process. Those who like to be creative will find facility planning a most absorbing process; those who find it difficult to be creative will probably never feel the satisfaction of creating a facility with innovative features. Creativity is not the exclusive possession of a favored few, but many librarians find it easy to be creative. By a program of reading widely and talking with successful library planners, everyone can increase the likelihood that he or she could devise some creative feature in a new library.

Obviously, creativity is not the only desirable quality to bring to the planning process. Good judgment and that elusive attribute, common sense, are just as important. A person could devise many creative features that might be absolute disasters because they lacked feasibility. For example, some clever but inexperienced librarian might get the idea for creating closed stacks for a special library, perhaps under the illusion that this innovative step would result in orderly shelves, with less time spent looking for misshelved books. The result would have been disastrous in the average special library, where quick access to the collection is an important feature. Admittedly this is an unlikely example, but perhaps it will suffice to show the need for seeking innovation coupled with a desire to make decisions that will stand the test of time. Choosing a red and green polka-dot color scheme for the library walls would certainly be creative, but it would hardly be advisable. So the planner is urged to seek both creative and sensible choices in the planning process.

Creative choices need not necessarily result in higher costs than routine choices. Chapter 9, for example, describes how a series of columns needed to support higher floors in a given library was used as a center for a number of rows of shelving surrounding each column, turning a liability into a ready-made, useful support for some much-needed, single-face shelving. In some cases creativity can actually save money. I once visited a new library in which there was a mezzanine floor around the edges of the reading room, with book stacks on the upper floor. Yet there was no way to move books to or from that level except by carrying them by hand. A book lift could have been installed at a modest cost when the library was being constructed. A little creativity and foresight on the part of the designers would have saved the library staff years of lugging books up and down by hand. Adding the lift after the library was completed would have been very costly.

BASIC STAGES OF PLANNING FACILITIES

There are many steps in the planning of a facility, but they can be reduced to a few basic stages for the purpose of aiding those unfamiliar with the process. Briefly put, they are as follows:

Pre-planning activities. This consists of preparation for the actual process of specific planning. The wise librarian does not wait until the process of planning a library is underway before beginning planning activities. There is much that can and should be done before conferring with architects and other professionals. This process includes gathering background information by visiting with librarians at other facilities, studying appropriate texts, or taking part in continuing education courses. Another important step is to analyze the needs of the library, consulting with library staff members and representatives of library users. See Chapter 6 for a discussion of this step.

Preparation of a library program. In the planning of facilities, the document that describes the nature of the library and its special needs is called a program. It gives the architects an insight into the type of library needed, including its goals, services, and future development. A prelude to preparation of this formal planning document would consist of gathering statistics on such topics as size of collection, rate of growth of each type of material (books versus journals, for example), estimated staff growth, and changing needs of the organization served. It is an indispensable step since a library is no better than the data upon which its plans are based. See Chapter 2 for a discussion of the preparation of a program. Chapters 7, 8 and 10 discuss the roles played by others on the typical planning team.

Space utilization. This consists of deciding on the location of different parts of the library—the stacks, staff space, user space, office equipment, etc. The environment in which each part would best be located is an important factor in the layout, such as keeping noisy equipment far enough away from study areas to avoid disturbing readers. Preparation of a layout is an important part of this step, leading to the architect's preparation of formal working drawings. See Chapter 3 for details on this process.

Selection of equipment and furnishings. The selection of the type and amount of equipment and furnishings plays a large role in the quality of a facility, making the difference between an unattractive, poorly furnished facility and an attractive, smoothly functioning unit. Selection of equipment that is cheaply made or poorly designed will haunt a library for years, long after the amount of money saved is long since forgotten. Great care must be taken to make suitable selections. See Chapters 4, 9 and 11 for more information on this topic.

Moving into a facility. The creation of a new or remodelled library usually involves the task of planning the move into the facility with the least amount of disruption of service. When skillfully done, users and staff all benefit and lost time is kept to a minimum. Chapter 5 is devoted to this topic.

DIFFERENCES AMONG TYPES OF LIBRARIES

Although it was previously stated that this book should be useful for planning special libraries in all types of settings, including the subject departments of academic and public libraries, it would be misleading to give the impression that planning say, a corporate library, would be identical to planning a map library in a university library system or a business department library that exists within a large public library. There are many differences, some of which should be pointed out.

One major difference is that most special libraries must include a technical services unit in which activities such as cataloging and acquisitions are carried on, whereas departmental libraries in public and academic libraries almost always rely on technical service units outside the department. Thus special libraries tend to require different kinds of staff areas and certain kinds of backup materials not located in subject departments of public or academic libraries.

Another difference is that most special libraries occupy space in buildings that they share with other parts of the organization, and the ultimate responsibility for the project usually rests on corporate managers who probably know little about special library facilities. Academic library units, particularly those devoted to a certain subject, such as chemistry or art, are also very often part of a larger building, which is planned by university officials who, as in the case of the corporate library, may or may not know much about libraries. Of course the top managers of the academic library system are involved in guiding the planning, but even they may have to defer to academic departments as to the type and size of library created. In contrast, public libraries are almost always separate buildings that are invariably planned by librarians. Clearly libraries planned by managers who are not themselves librarians present extra problems.

Public and academic departmental subject libraries have the rest of the library system to fall back on as far as extra space or perhaps materials of limited interest are concerned, whereas most special libraries have no other part of the organization to serve as a backup unit and no other source close at hand for materials of secondary interest.

As far as budgets are concerned, all types of libraries are apt to be subject to decisions made by upper echelons of management, such as boards, executive committees or high-ranking officials. One difference is that the board governing a public library might be more familiar with the problems and needs of libraries than a board of trustees at a university or the executive board of a manufacturing company. However, the fund raising campaigns of public libraries can be more uncertain of success than is the funding promised to the library by an executive committee within an organization. The ability of the library manager to convince decision-makers of the worth of the library can play a large role in the amount of money available for the facility being planned, no matter what kind of library is involved.

In Chapters 2 through 5 the basic steps named above will be discussed in a concise, simplified manner. Further elaboration on most of these topics will be found in Part II.

As previously mentioned, Chapter 12 consists of a sizable number of references recommended for further study. However, if only one text were to be named as being outstanding, it would undoubtedly be the recent revision of the classic work by Keyes Metcalf.[1] Although aimed at those planning academic and research libraries, its thorough coverage of a multitude of topics and its reliability make it a useful book for all library planners.

REFERENCE

1. Metcalf, Keyes D. *Planning academic and research library buildings*. Second edition by Philip D. Leighton and David C. Weber. Chicago: American Library Association; 1986. 630p.

A comprehensive treatment of all aspects of library planning. Includes numerous drawings, sample library layouts, and sample library programs. Highly recommended.

Chapter 2

Preparing the Library Program

The building program statement, sometimes called simply the library program, is an essential document for planning a library. Its purpose is to define the type of library desired, its goals, the size of the collection, the amount of space needed, etc. It should be considered flexible, so that the program reflects changing ideas about the library, even if certain basic statistics it contains are not changed.

CONTENTS OF A LIBRARY PROGRAM

Although no two library programs are alike, the following topics are commonly included in the average program:

General Features

Objectives of the library. What are the goals of the library and what effect do they have on its design?

Type of library. Is the library a place where serious retrospective research is done by its users, or are most of its services aimed at providing current data quickly? Are there other characteristics that describe its role in the organization?

Status of the library. Is the library newly developed and growing at a fast pace, or is it on a plateau of growth? Are there other library services that may be added in the near future? Is it likely new responsibilities will be given the library, such as care of organizational records?

Location of the library. What sort of location would benefit the library the most? What other activities or departments would profit the most by proximity to the library?

Nature of Library Users

Number and types of users. How many potential users are there and what percentage do they constitute of different user groups, such as professional, managerial, clerical?

User activities. What sort of activities take place in the organization served by the library, such as research, marketing, production, or administrative oversight?

Type of library use. Do most users make personal visits to the library as contrasted with relying primarily on the telephone or sending their assistants to conduct library business? Do many users need the library for non-library purposes, such as writing reports, conferring with colleagues, or seeking a change of pace from the pressure of work?

Construction Features

Length of useful service of the facility. For how many years should the new facility serve before it would be outgrown? How would expansion be facilitated at that time?

Unusual construction features. Are there any special demands to be made on the structure, such as greater than usual floor loading (measured in the number of pounds per square foot the floor will support)? Will special entrances and exits be required due to local ordinances? Will there be a need for special areas, such as a vault for sensitive documents or for archival materials? Will structural pillars and support columns need prescribed spacing to accommodate library stacks without wasting space?

Environmental controls. What temperature and humidity conditions will be required? Will conditions depend upon the type and amount of equipment (like computers) in the library? What acoustical conditions would be required? Will at least some of the windows in the library be operable so that there would be outside air available in the event of a shutdown of the heating, ventilating, and air conditioning (HVAC) system?

Handicapped people. Will there be any special construction features needed to enable handicapped people to use the library without undue difficulty?

Space Requirements

Collection space. How much space will be required to house the collection for the estimated length of service of the library? What types of materials will be kept (periodicals, monographs, technical reports, etc.) and in what quantities? Will they require special types of containers or stacks? Will there be any possibility of a storage area outside the library for little-used materials? Will there be any change in the availability of literature from sources outside the library? Will compact storage devices like laser disks and microforms reduce the amount of space needed?

Staff space. How much space will be required for work areas for the library staff? What sort of environmental conditions will the work areas require (such as differing levels of lighting, electrical outlets, or telephone jacks)? Are the space needs for computers, word processors, terminals, and other equipment amply planned for? Is there space for supplies, staff coats, book trucks, and related devices?

User space. How much space will be required for seating library users? What different types of seating and work areas would be required? Are separate conference rooms or rooms for user instruction being considered?

Services Offered

User services. Do user services include the ones commonly associated with special libraries, such as reference service, current awareness service, interlibrary loan service, and assistance to writers and editors? Is the library involved in translating foreign documents? Does the library assist in a regular review of current literature? Are any new services planned or are any present services being discontinued? Is there any interest in purchasing from outside sources services now performed by the staff?

Technical services. What are the means of access to the library's collection and outside sources of information, such as catalogs (manual or online), special indexes, thesauri and other finding tools, including access to bibliographic utilities? Are materials processed, indexed or cataloged on the premises? Is any move likely toward purchase from outside sources of services now performed by the staff? Does the library purchase literature from outside sources as a service for individuals and departments in the organization?

Records management. Is the library responsible for the care and organization of organizational records, such as current files, archives, correspondence and the like? Is such a responsibility likely to be given the library in the future?

TOPICS RELATED TO PROGRAM PREPARATION

As can be seen from the above checklist, preparing a good program is not done quickly. It includes a careful collection of data, and it requires working cooperatively with others involved in the project.

Gathering Statistics

The better the data available on the present status of the library, the better the program will be. If a librarian has only a vague idea about the size and rate of growth of a collection, for example, the projection of what to plan for will also be inexact. While no one is apt to have completely accurate statistics, there are certain standards of accuracy required for preparing a library program if it is to have real value to the librarian and the other planners. As described above, a rather large number of topics is involved. Thus statistics should include collection size, number of potential users, amount of service given (reference use, technical service output, current awareness service, etc.). For those not yet involved in planning, it is better to keep statistics on a more or less regular basis over the years than to rush around madly at the last minute. Statistics kept over a number of years will also be of greater value than figures based only on current use.

The Planning Team

The librarian will be working with several others during the planning process (although preparing the library program is almost exclusively the responsibility of the library representative). A full description of the planning team will be found in Chapter 7, so only a brief discussion is given here.

One of the most important persons will be the architect (unless the project is very small, such as making rather minor modifications in an existing library). The architect's knowledge or lack of knowledge about planning libraries will probably come to light early in the process. If the architect claims experience in this type of project, it is in order to ask to see examples of his or her libraries. If the architect has no such experience, show the architect examples of good books on the subject, such as those cited in the bibliography in Chapter 12. Another professional commonly found on the planning team is the interior designer. Still another member of the team may be a professional consultant. As in the case of selecting architects, it is important for the planning team to check the references of all professionals and see evidence of libraries in which they were involved in planning. More information about the roles of the architect and the interior designer will be found in Chapters 8 and 10. The work of the consultant is discussed in Chapter 7.

Inevitably there will be several individuals from the sponsoring company or organization who are assigned to the planning process. One of them might well be technically trained, such as a building engineer, who would be qualified to evaluate technical aspects, including ventilation systems, fire regulations, and floor loading requirements. Someone else on the team may represent the interests of top executives, including projected costs and time schedules. The larger the sponsoring organization the more members there are apt to be on the team.

Naturally, plans for a new facility must be acceptable to one's supervisor before the process is very far along. If the librarian and the librarian's supervisor are far apart on what should be done, there are bound to be some unpleasant experiences during the planning at all stages. A willingness to accept certain design features that aren't to one's liking is almost a necessity in most cases. Major issues are probably worth the librarian's presenting all the evidence he or she can muster to influence decisions, but it is foolish to make a big fuss over minor points.

It is generally advisable for the librarian to hire a consultant to help in various stages of the planning process, especially if the librarian is inexperienced in library planning. Lists of library building consultants are maintained by the American Library Association and the Special Libraries Association. Whoever represents the interests of the library on the planning team must be well informed and prepared to speak up for the features important to the library. Even when consultants are used, they may not be part of every meeting of the planning team, leaving the library representative as the only voice for the library. It is no place for a shrinking violet nor for an intemperate person. Undue shyness or overbearing gruffness are both poor qualities for any member of the team to exhibit. A sense of humor and an ability to recognize when to compromise are invaluable tools for the planner.

In summary, the preparation of a library program calls for informed decisions based on as much information and careful study as is feasible. It also calls for smooth relationships with the members of the planning team. Even then there will be features of the final plan that may be disappointing, but hard work in the preplanning stage and the program preparation stage will help keep such features to a minimum.

Chapter 3

Space Utilization

One of the most important steps in planning a library is preparing the layout or schematic design that shows the location and amount of space allotted to each part of the library, e.g., for the librarian's office, the photocopiers, and the stacks for periodicals. Sometimes called space utilization, the creation of a good layout is usually a repetitive process in which the plans gradually achieve greater suitability and acceptability to the planning team. Although the use of computers by many architectural firms has brought an element of speed and flexibility to the process, there is still no foolproof, easy method of making a creative, satisfactory layout. It takes time, much thought, and usually several preliminary versions before the process is completed. Even then unexpected problems may arise and require changes to be made.

There are at least four aspects of space utilization that must be considered in preparing a layout, namely, a determination of the amount of space required, consideration of the best environment for a given activity or piece of equipment, a check on the costs involved in various choices, and an awareness of esthetic aspects, so that the library is as attractive as possible. The following pages describe these four factors and show how they affect the preparation of a layout.

PREPARATION OF FLOOR PLANS

Space Requirements

A critical step in the process of preparing a program is the calculation of the amount of space needed for the staff, for library users, and for the collections. While there are some other components to plan for in a typical library, these three constitute the bulk of the space requirements. The care and skill with which this part of the program is prepared will have a great impact on the quality of the layout. Later in this chapter some figures are given for calculating space.

Miscalculations of space could be a fatal flaw in any library, particularly if the errors are not discovered until work is underway. Therefore it is important to check and recheck these calculations before proceeding very far. One of the important services provided by consultants is that of ensuring the accuracy of the calculations for space needs. A consultant would, for example, see that space needs for the collection are broken down into the required number of categories, such as reference volumes, bound periodicals, unbound periodicals, monographs (or books), technical reports, drawings, microfiche, maps, etc., together with a calculation of the rate of growth anticipated for each type of material. Some may be relatively dormant in growth, while periodicals, for example, might be growing at a remarkably high rate. A lump sum of pieces to house is useless without breaking down the total into categories such as these and estimating growth rates for each category.

Over the years certain standard recommendations regarding the proper allocation of space for the average library have evolved, changing as new and improved library equipment is created or as the needs of people change. The following checklist should provide useful data for planning the average special library:

Shelving. Bookstacks are either single-faced or double-faced. In planning for their ultimate capacity, it is unwise to expect to use every available inch on each shelf. Some authorities recommend planning so that the average shelf is only 80 percent full, thus building some leeway in the calculations. Also it is difficult to add or remove books when a shelf is filled to capacity. The average thickness of books varies from thin monographs to large bound periodical volumes. The recommendations take this into account. Table 3.1 is a conservative estimate of the space needed for shelving various kinds of books.

Assumptions: Shelves are three feet in length; a double-faced stack unit has a base shelf and six movable shelves per side; stacks are filled to 80 percent of capacity; and there is a 36-inch aisle between stack rows.

TABLE 3.1. Shelving Capacity

	Vols./shelf	Vols./double-faced stack	Vols./sq. ft.
Monographs	14	200	13
Reference Books	12	170	11
Bound Journals	12	170	11

It should be noted these are conservative figures, using only 80 percent of the capacity of the shelves. In making actual calculations, some readers may find the figure for the capacity per double-faced stack unit easier to use than the volumes per square foot figure. Aisle widths different than those used in the example or books that are consistently different in thickness than those in the example would obviously result in capacities that differ from this table.

Current periodicals may be placed in periodical display stacks, averaging three per row. Flat shelving of issues allows for many more per shelf, but then only the spines of the issues would be visible.

Heights of shelving range from 42 inches (waist-high) to 90 inches. A fully loaded double-faced section with seven shelves on each side weighs 725 lb. with wooden shelving and 800–900 lb. with metal shelving. For most purposes shelves measuring at least 10 inches from front to back are recommended, although both smaller and larger sizes are available. (Some manufacturers express shelf depth in what is called "nominal" sizes, which are one inch larger than the actual measurement of the depth. It is important that the planner be sure what the manufacturer means by describing shelves of a certain depth.) See also Chapter 9 for a discussion of shelf sizes.

The width of aisles between ranges of stacks varies depending on factors such as the number of users, the popularity of the material shelved or the amount of space available. When there is an abundance of space, aisles 3 feet wide are usually recommended, with 4-foot aisles for very busy sections. On the other hand, if there are severe space restrictions, or if the amount of traffic is not expected to be great, aisles could conceivably be reduced to 30 inches. (It should be noted this spacing would increase the storage capacity of a given range of shelving by 10 percent versus that obtained with 36-inch aisles.) In storage areas not accessible to the public, 30-inch aisles would be acceptable.

In recent years movable shelving, which allows stack units to be pushed close together or separated for access, has become more popular. Several types are currently manufactured. Detailed information about the construction and utilization of standard and movable shelving is given in Chapter 9.

Vertical files. Vertical files for letter-size paper average around 30 inches deep and 15 inches wide, whereas files for legal-size paper are 18 inches wide. Many librarians favor files that are arranged sidewise (called lateral files), measuring about 36 inches wide and 18 inches deep. An important aspect in planning locations for files is the amount of space required for opening the drawers. For vertical files the distance from the back of the cabinet to the front of a fully open drawer is about 52 inches; whereas it is only about 36 inches for a lateral file. Files are available with various numbers of drawers, ranging from one to five drawers in height. The latter is recommended for libraries where there are large quantities of material to be filed; those with modest requirements might prefer two- or three-drawer models, which fit conveniently beside a desk. Whatever size is selected, frames are highly recommended to allow file folders to hang; the ease of filing and retrieval this equipment provides is well worth the extra expense.

Microform storage units. Microforms are usually stored in special metal cabinets made to fit the dimensions of microfiche or microfilm reels.

Microfilm cabinets come in a range of sizes, with five to eleven drawers. A typical cabinet is around 30 inches deep and 24 inches wide. An eleven-drawer cabinet can hold 1500 reels of 16 mm. microfilm and weighs around 700 pounds when fully loaded.

Microfiche cabinets also come in a variety of heights, ranging from five to ten drawers. They average around 30 inches deep and

22 inches wide. A ten-drawer unit would hold about 130,000 fiche of 5 mil thickness, weighing about 700 pounds fully loaded.

It is obvious that microforms offer very compact storage but the floor loading should be at least 150 lb./sq. ft. A microfilm cabinet as described above would require a floor loading of 140 lb./sq. ft. while a microfiche cabinet would be a bit more. Some manufacturers recommend placing these cabinets on basement levels or ground floor levels if 150 lb./sq. ft. is not feasible.

Furniture spacing. There are no universally accepted standards for the amount of space required for common items of furniture, but the figures given in Table 3.2 have been found useful by many special library planners.

TABLE 3.2. Furniture Space Recommendations

Aisles	Center or main aisles: 4–4.5 ft.
	Between tables and wall: 5 ft.
	Between tables, if chairs are back to back: 5–6 ft.
	Between single tables: 4 ft.
	Between table ends without chairs: 3.5–4 ft.
	Between vertical files, if facing: 6 ft.
	Between bookstacks: 3 ft. (more for heavy traffic)
Areas	In front of circulation desk: 6 ft.
	In front of card catalog (or terminal): 5 ft.
	In front of reference desk: 5–6 ft.

Work areas (staff and users). The amount of space needed by a staff member or by a library user depends somewhat upon the nature of the library and the nature of the particular activities of the user. A cataloger, for example, normally needs room for book trucks or shelves for work in progress, while a reference librarian needs a computer terminal plus shelving of major reference works at his or her fingertips. A map user would certainly need far more room at a table or carrel than a reader with a monograph or periodical issue. Those who want to browse through current journals might need only a comfortable chair without requiring a table. Generalizations are thus not reliable guides.

The general estimates in Table 3.3 will probably need adjustments upward or downward, depending upon the particular situation.

TABLE 3.3. Work Station Space Recommendations

Reading area	25 sq. ft. per reader, with more required in certain types of research. A carrel housing a microform reader or a computer would require 30/35 sq. per reader.
Staff area	100–125 sq. ft. per person, with 150 sq. ft. needed for technical service areas. Library managers should have at least 150 sq. ft. (in an enclosed area to allow for privacy).

Environmental Factors

It is not enough simply to have space for all of the various components needed in a library. The location of these components is extremely important. For example, placing the area where library users will sit to do reading and research immediately next to busy telephones or noisy photocopiers would be a mistake. Or placing the terminal for the online catalog directly in the path of incoming traffic would make its use awkward. Many considerations affect the choice of locations of most components of the library. The best test of how well one has considered environmental aspects is whether the layout will actually work successfully when it is put into use. Unfortunately it is usually too late to correct mistakes by that time.

It is rare if a perfect location could be found for each part of the library; trade-offs are part of planning. Often factors that favor one position for a particular part of the library upset the proposed location for other library units, so that compromises must be sought. The main point to remember is to make the trade-offs as sensible and creative as possible.

A list of considerations that affect location of units might be useful at this point:

Noise. This is a vital factor to consider. Areas where library users are located should be kept as quiet as possible. Placing users next to photocopiers or staff work areas (where ringing of telephones and conversation are normal and necessary) are prime examples of bad locations. Sometimes creative planners have found ways to use stack areas to block out the sound from reaching study areas. The stacks need not be full height, even waist-high units would help.

Some schools of thought favor open work areas for staff areas partly because the cost of constructing walls around many work stations is eliminated and partly for esthetic reasons. Whatever the reason, the effect of noise from staff operations on users should not be overlooked. Also the value of a certain amount of privacy for supervisors must not be ignored. Supervising people requires confidential communication with them. I once worked in a library where my office was so open (it had a four-foot high glass wall around it) that I had to take the employees I supervised out into a stairwell whenever anything of a confidential nature had to be discussed. Needless to say, it was far from satisfactory.

Traffic. The movement of people into, out of and around the library must be considered so that the areas where there would be the most traffic are kept relatively unencumbered. Both efficiency and safety require careful planning along this line. Also users trying to concentrate at tables and carrels are bound to be adversely affected by a constant movement of numbers of people past the study area. A certain amount of traffic is almost unavoidable unless one is considering individual study rooms, which are often desirable and feasible. Chapter 11 discusses such rooms in some detail.

Library areas that should be carefully planned with the effect of the movement of people in mind include the space in front of the circulation counter, areas around computer terminals, areas around microform readers, and areas next to study carrels and tables.

Convenience. Certain parts of the library are used so much that it would be terribly inconvenient for the staff and for users if these parts were located in some out-of-the-way place. For example, card catalogs or terminals for online catalogs must be located in a convenient place, yet out of the heaviest traffic. So again the question of trade-offs arises. The most convenient place for a card or online catalog might be right in front of the library entrance, but this would put it in a very bad spot, blocking traffic. So the usual solution is to make the catalog near the entrance but to one side of the areas needed for aisles.

Although circulation records and the monitoring of users as they leave the library are not nearly as important in most special libraries as they are in public and academic libraries, it is still wise to have the circulation desk fairly near the entrance (again, not blocking the aisles) if for no other reason than to have a staff person readily available for answering inquiries by library users. These questions might often be referred to reference librarians located further away from the entrance, but at least users don't have to wander around before finding a human being to talk to. Making it difficult to reach staff members responsible for user service gives a library the appearance of being indifferent to user needs. Yet the reader service staff, particularly reference librarians, should also have a reasonable amount of privacy for doing the research and study they carry on. It is not essential that those in technical services be easily accessible to the public.

Cost Factors

There are many ways of spending a lot of money in creating a library that have little to do with the quality of the library. This includes library layouts. A lavishly designed library layout is not necessarily a good layout. For example, leaving huge aisles between library stacks would usually be a waste of space, as would be the allocation of unusually large work areas for staff members and users. Several other examples could be given, such as the choice of custom-made windows or inefficient configuration of walls and staircases. In addition, some features which appear to provide cost savings may well cost more in the long run.

For example, the plans for many libraries locate lighting fixtures in the stack areas running parallel to the stack ranges. This is fine if the fixtures are actually in the middle of the aisles between the stacks and if the stacks will never be moved. But more than one librarian has found that the fixtures were not installed exactly in the middle of the aisles, for various reasons that occurred during the construction process. A better option in many cases might be to install the rows of lighting fixtures perpendicular to the stacks.

Then no matter where the stacks might be moved later, the light is still overhead in the aisles. Also the rather delicate placement of the lighting fixtures is avoided since making them perpendicular to the stacks would not require the precision required to locate them exactly in the middle of stack aisles. It should be noted, however, that some planners believe perpendicular lighting makes it difficult to examine books on bottom shelves.

Still another example of cost effectiveness involves the selection of the type of carpet for the library. Although most special libraries routinely include carpeting now because of its attractiveness, its greater comfort for walking, and its sound absorption, there are mistakes made in the name of reducing costs that actually cost more over the years. For example, the top administration may favor installing the same sort of carpet throughout the entire building in an effort to save costs. This may result in using a type of carpet totally unsuited for the library. Experience has shown that carpeting that is light in color shows soil much more than a darker shade, and carpeting that has no pattern shows soil and every scrap of paper dropped on it much more than a pattern, such as a tweed. I have visited relatively new libraries in which light-colored patternless carpeting was used, and it was already unbelievably shoddy looking. So what might be suitable for relatively low traffic areas could turn out to be a poor choice for a busy library. Carpeting can be installed in individual squares, which simplifies replacement of worn spots.

The advice of architects, interior designers and specialists in certain specific areas will help the planner avoid many obvious pitfalls as far as costs are concerned, but do not be surprised if you have to convince some of these professionals of the value of your ideas. They may be very skilled in their work but might never have thought carefully about every idea that librarians propose. Librarians and professional planners can usually learn from each other. See Chapter 10 for more information on this topic.

Esthetic Factors

While environmental aspects have a lot to do with making a given layout workable, other factors should be kept in mind so that the library will be attractive and pleasant. For example, placing a study table in a corner so that readers sitting there have only bare walls to stare at is far less satisfactory than placing it near an outside window. The attractiveness of a library can also be spoiled by the placement of certain mundane, utilitarian objects and activities in a prominent place. Areas for handling the mail for example, are certainly vital to the operation of a special library, but that doesn't mean they should be located adjacent to the front desk area, the first part of the library seen by most visitors.

Some library managers have a knack for adding the little touches that make a library much more attractive. In some organizations there are quite stringent rules about such things as including live plants to the library. I visited one such library recently and was told by the library manager that her firm had two standard plants, known as "corporate plants" in that company, from which to choose. There was even an official plant caretaker who made regular visits to keep the plants watered. Situations of this sort tend to stifle creativity, although one can understand the cost-cutting features of such a system.

Closets for the storage of supplies as well as clothes closets for use by the staff are often details that get overlooked in the complex process of completing a library layout. They are essential, however, if the library is to be kept free of clutter and unsightly storage.

Safety Factors

One of the prime responsibilities of architects, interior designers and building engineers is to see that the library plans meet all applicable requirements for safety, including fire regulations and the recommendations of safety experts. Theoretically the librarian would have little to contribute on these topics, but it would be well for him or her to examine proposed layouts carefully to see if any problem area escaped notice. Recently I visited a new library built for a prominent law firm and was told that the library was quite far along before anyone noticed there was no fire exit, commonly required by city ordinances in many libraries. One wonders how such a basic element could have been overlooked.

One area in which the librarian might make a contribution involves storage of library materials. Vertical files, for example, can be lethal if they are placed so that a person turning into an aisle containing them could trip over a drawer that was pulled out into the aisle. One remedy is to plan aisles so that drawers will not be close enough to the ends of the aisles to allow such an accident. Sidewise files diminish this problem, but many libraries still use the type with drawers that pull out.

As for the stacks, it is the responsibility of the manufacturer and the installer to see that they are properly anchored to the floor and otherwise properly installed. If movable shelving is involved, the librarian might do well to see that the floor is perfectly level to ensure ease of operation. The safety features of movable shelving should have been carefully tested long before installation, although a careful check of its operation should be made before the equipment and installation are accepted and signed for.

Closely related to safety is the consideration that must be given to access for handicapped people. Many states have laws requiring easy access for those who are in wheelchairs or are otherwise handicapped. This may apply in some cases to special libraries if they serve the general public. Architects should be well aware of these requirements.

DRAWING FLOOR PLANS

Many librarians look upon the preparation of an actual floor plan with uneasiness, often because they feel they have no talent at drawing. This is a needless worry, because useful layouts can be prepared by anyone who is careful and neat. Freehand drawing is not required since most of the process involves drawing straight lines with rulers or drawing around templates to show more complicated figures.

Once the calculations described above have been completed, the next step is to obtain some graph paper for preliminary sketches. A useful type of paper is on a scale of one-quarter of an inch equaling one foot, although similar scales would probably work just as well.

Before a line is drawn on the paper, the planner should have already roughly determined how many square feet would be needed to house the three main parts of the library: the area needed for the collection, the area for staff members, and the area for users. In most cases the librarian may have been assigned an area of a given size and told to make do with that. In more enlightened situations, the librarian has the luxury of making preliminary sketches and determining the ideal amount of space required. In such a case, there should be no problem fitting everything into the assigned area, but if the librarian is simply assigned a given amount of space without his or her estimate being considered, it is a case of somehow trying to fit as much as is essential into the allotted area.

Assuming the latter case, once the total figures for collections, staff areas and user areas are compared with the total space allotted, then the planner will see at once how well the space will accommodate everything desired for the library. Usually something will have to be reduced in area or even eliminated. Trade-offs will be made once again since any single feature to be considered for elimination or reduction in size will probably have to be compared with other features that should face reconsideration. It is sometimes a painful process to have to cut back or discard a favorite feature.

Once the rough fit is achieved, the main question is to decide what to put where, keeping the factors previously discussed, such as noise, convenience, and safety, in mind. The next step would be to sketch in lightly the possible locations for the stacks, the main staff work areas and the main user seating areas, avoiding detailed locations until satisfied the general location is suitable. For example, there is no point in carefully drawing in 25 rows of stacks before it is quite clear where the stacks should be. This does not mean that changes will never have to be made even after a lot of the basic decisions have been made. Sometimes it is difficult to see just how the parts will fit together until a certain amount of detail has been drawn in.

Librarians are often unaware of the value of using small templates or patterns for drawing in such features as tables, chairs, or stack units. Some manufacturers of library furniture or firms that sell library supplies have kits available for the use by planners. A typical kit includes one or two plastic sheets with cutouts for everything from charging desks to round tables. Some even show recommended distances between pieces of furniture or formulas for calculating shelving capacities. If such kits are not available for some reason, one temporary substitute could be cardboard templates made by the planner. However, this takes time, and the homemade patterns do not work as well as plastic templates.

As things gradually fall into place, detailed drawings should be made of each element of furniture or equipment. Having made decisions previously about relationships, such as what would be next to a row of windows, or what would be placed near the entrance, will speed up the process of drawing the layout. It is just as well to keep working with pencil until decisions stand the test of a second or third examination by the planner and favorable comments from others. Then going over the lines with ink makes it ready to show outsiders, such as supervisors, members of a library advisory committee, etc. Undoubtedly other layouts will have to be drawn; it would be rare to get agreement from others on a first attempt. Different versions should be dated and kept until the project is completed. Some of them should be kept in a folder containing a history of the project, not only for the organization's archives but as an aid to the planner should another project come along.

Some librarians have difficulty in visualizing what a two-dimensional drawing would look like in a three-dimensional world. It is necessary to be able to realize what a plan would look like if adopted. Computer technology has come to the rescue of planners with this problem. Modern architectural firms have for several years routinely used special computers to prepare a two-dimensional drawing, then, at the request of a client, to convert the drawing into a rendition that shows three dimensions. Such a service would be an item to look for in determining whether or not to use a particular architectural firm. An example of the conversion of a sketch into a three-dimensional drawing can be found in Chapter 10.

This chapter has shown the reader the many steps in deciding how space will be used. The next chapter is concerned with selecting equipment and furniture.

Chapter 4

Selection of Equipment and Furnishings

A cleverly designed library with a splendid collection and an unusual decor can still prove to be disappointing to its users and the library staff if the equipment and furnishings are not suitable, adequate, or attractive. The selection of what goes into the library can have a great impact on how it is perceived by those who use it. This chapter discusses the topic briefly, with references to other chapters that deal with the subject in greater detail. Chapter 11 "Furnishing the Electronic Library" is primarily concerned with this subject, including making provision for computers and other electronic equipment.

Many librarians use interior designers, whose services include advising clients on the selection of furniture and certain equipment. Their knowledge of materials, methods of construction of furnishings, selection of colors, and placement of items all contribute to creating a library that is not only attractive but also very functional. Furthermore, their advice helps the untrained librarian avoid shoddy selections that would soon prove unwise choices. Something that may appeal to an untrained eye might not hold up as well over the years as an item selected by a trained person. Most libraries are planned for long-term use, so that durability of items is very important. For more information on the role of interior designers, see Chapter 10.

Several factors enter into a decision as to what furniture and equipment to buy including: cost, appearance, ability to perform adequately, durability, size, availability, reputation of the vendor, ease of repair or adjustments that might be needed. Entire articles have been written on the selection of just one item, such as bookstacks, or computers, or furniture. It would be folly to do more than touch on some aspects of the subject in this chapter. One very useful book on the subject is by Pierce, a monograph about furnishing library interiors.[1]

There are a few basic pointers, however, that should be kept in mind in the selection process. One is the desirability of visiting furniture and equipment showrooms or other libraries to see actual items, not just handsome photographs or drawings. There is no substitute for this process, and seeing an item up close may either strengthen one's enthusiasm for it or else make undetected flaws become obvious. Asking the opinions of librarians who own the equipment is, of course, also useful, but not a substitute for seeing it in person. Before getting to this point, however, it is often helpful to read reliable reports about various brands of products. One such reliable source is *Library Technology Reports*, a bimonthly publication that centers on a particular product each issue, such as PBX telephone systems for libraries or computerized circulation control systems.[2]

FURNITURE

The selection of bookstacks represents a major percentage of the total cost of furnishing a library. As previously mentioned, choices include all-metal shelving, all-wood (or wood substitute) shelving, combinations of metal and wood, and movable shelving. Each has its merits. Wood shelving tends to be more attractive but undoubtedly costs more than all-metal shelving. Metal shelving is more common in large libraries, though designers of plush libraries in which the appearance of warmth is important often prefer wood shelving (or at least wood end panels) to all-metal shelving. Several special types of shelving are common, such as those designed to display current periodical issues, those equipped with hanging folders for current issues of newspapers, or those with metal backs to the shelves and slots to hold metal dividers (for thin items like technical reports). A detailed analysis of the features and construction of all types of shelving is found in Chapter 9.

Chairs and tables (and variants such as carrels) offer many choices for the planners. Besides style and size, such factors as comfort and durability are important. Tables in general tend to be smaller, often designed to serve one person, whereas years ago it was common to see long tables that would seat a dozen or more people. Evidently the need for privacy while working in libraries is more important to users. However, each library should have at least one table that could easily accommodate four people since users occasionally need to consult with others. Also a larger table would better accommodate maps or large volumes.

The use of carrels ensures even greater privacy, and some libraries allow users to leave materials in the carrel for a day or so without items being disturbed. Some carrels are efficiently designed so that four people can each sit without anyone else in view; yet the four-person carrel occupies less space than that needed for four individual carrels. For even greater privacy, the use of separate study rooms is not uncommon. In some cases computer facilities are best placed in separate rooms.

Care must be taken in planning carrels to make sure that the proper type and number of electric outlets are provided. Many libraries want to install computers or terminals in carrels, as well as microform readers. The same situation holds for any enclosed rooms and for staff members' desks.

Chairs range greatly in size and comfort. Most special libraries have a small area where current periodicals can be perused by people who come in just for that purpose. It is common to have comfortable, upholstered chairs in such an area. They make the process of glancing over periodicals inviting and pleasant. They are not designed for use over long periods of time, as would be the case for readers at carrels or formal library tables. A small, low table in the middle of the browsing area is another common feature that makes the area more informal and appealing.

Chairs at tables and carrels should be carefully selected so as to match the height of the table top. I have seen carelessly selected arm chairs that were so mismatched that the arms were too high to allow them to slide under the table. Readers could not get their chairs closer to the table than the front edge of the arm. Another feature to consider in chairs is how easily they may be tipped back. Some readers prefer to tilt chairs back, which can damage the chairs and endanger the readers. Fortunately many chairs are designed so that it is practically impossible to tilt them back too far.

Floor coverings have been limited in recent years to two

choices—vinyl tiles and carpeting. The advantages of carpeting include providing greater comfort for those who walk about on them a great deal and absorbing sound. There is no question that carpeted libraries are more comfortable to walk in and are quieter than those with vinyl tiles. It is difficult to compare the relative costs of carpeting and tiles since the quality of each can vary so much. If carpeting is selected, keep in mind the comments previously made about the tendency of light tones of colors to show soil much more than darker shades as well as the fact that carpeting without a pattern also shows soil and wear more quickly than a patterned carpet.

EQUIPMENT

Modern libraries normally contain many types of equipment, some of which was either unknown or little used until fairly recently. Today it is taken for granted that a special library will contain one or more computers and printers, a microfiche reader/printer, a photocopier, perhaps a CD-ROM player, and possibly a facsimile machine. Each has been the subject of periodical articles and books, so that only a few basic principles are needed here.

In selecting or considering equipment, some points to keep in mind are as follows:

Performance. No matter how inexpensive or readily available an item may be, the manner in which a piece of equipment operates, its merits, and its drawbacks, are far more important aspects to consider than total cost. If one piece of equipment easily outdistances its rivals, it is usually false economy to purchase a lesser brand because of cost alone. If equipment doesn't provide the service needed, no amount of saving on prices is worthwhile.

While the majority of salespersons are completely honest, it is wise to arrange for visits to former clients of the salesperson to examine in detail the performance of the equipment, bearing in mind that performance requirements differ among libraries.

Product reliability. The ability of equipment to provide trouble-free service over a long time period is important to libraries, who usually do not have the funds to replace equipment frequently. Information about reliability is not easy to obtain, but owners of the type of equipment being considered could be asked about this point.

Some repairmen are occasionally able to evaluate the reliability of equipment, based on what their experience has been in making repairs. A long warranty period covering major parts of the equipment is another protection against expensive repairs.

Maintenance contracts. Aside from repairs, the periodic inspection, cleaning, and routine servicing that much equipment needs can often be handled by annual service contracts that save money versus having to pay maintenance people to come in on a special call each time they are needed. Points to consider are the dependability of the firm and the quality of their work, both points again calling for checking with their customers.

Delivery and installation schedules. It is important to have firm dates for delivery of equipment and its installation. Since delays in arrival of major equipment could badly upset library planning, the possibility of penalty clauses in the contract might well be considered. Bookstacks are one of the key items whose delay could wreck completion schedules. Many librarians can vouch for the havoc caused by delayed stack installations.

It is clear that there are many considerations to keep in mind in selecting equipment and furnishings. No doubt the reader will readily think of other points that affect the important process of making these choices.

REFERENCES

1. Pierce, William S. *Furnishing the library interior*. New York: Dekker; 1980. 288p.

A thorough discussion of the process of selecting furniture and equipment for all types of libraries. Evaluation of possible choices, methods of construction, and placement of furniture are some of the topics covered.

2. *Library Technology Reports*. Chicago: American Library Association; 1965– . Bimonthly.

A reliable source of information about all sorts of library furniture and equipment. Independent laboratory testing is done, and expert evaluators prepare analyses of the products. Topics range from computerized systems to photocopiers. Each issue is devoted to a single topic or product.

Chapter 5

Moving the Library

It would be a rare case if a new library were created and there were no books and materials to move in. Invariably the process of designing a new or remodeled library includes the need to plan for the move into it. Like all other aspects of library planning, the move could be done smoothly if planned carefully. It also could be a very disorganized, time-consuming, frustrating process if it is not planned carefully. The purpose of this chapter is to provide guidance in making the move an efficient, smooth-running operation.

SELECTION OF A MOVING COMPANY

Except for tiny libraries that have access to an adequate source of manual laborers or maintenance workers, libraries are moved by commercial firms. The company that is chosen should have had experience in moving libraries. This is a point that should not be taken for granted. Find out what libraries the company has moved and talk to the librarians whose libraries were involved. It is easy for a moving company to claim experience it has not had.

Assuming that the firm has had experience, the librarian must work closely with the company, discussing the following points:

Schedules. Determine when they could do the job, ask about working on a weekend (and what extra costs would be involved in weekend work, if any) and how many person hours would be required to make the move (after you have prepared your statistics on what is to be moved).

Equipment. What sort of containers would be used for books? Either boxes (cardboard or wood) or hand trucks of various types are generally the choices available. The containers should not be so large as to make lifting and carrying of them unduly difficult. They must be sturdy enough to withstand the rigors of a move. If possible, containers should be designed so that one can be stacked on top of another securely, facilitating stacking them on dollies or trucks. If rolling trucks are to be used, their wheels should be large enough to make it easy to move them over carpeting. Some librarians favor the use of sturdy carts having 4-foot long shelves on each side. The shelves are securely fastened to the base of the cart. (They can be visualized as two book cases stacked back-to-back on casters.)

PREPARATIONS FOR THE MOVE

The librarian, or his or her staff member appointed for the duty, bears the responsibility for determining what is to be moved. This includes not only what specific items are involved but also the quantities of items to move. For example, a decision might be made not to move certain old periodicals; this must be decided before the calculation of volumes to move is made. Certain steps should be made as soon as possible, rather than waiting till the move is imminent.

Weeding the collection. There is no point in moving materials that are of little value, so it is important to decide what can be left behind early in the process. Ideally it should be decided before the library program is completed, as the amount of space needed for shelving could be considerably affected if large amounts of materials are not to be moved. Often a library may drift along for years keeping little-used materials, but when a new library is planned there is no excuse for not evaluating the entire collection to determine what is no longer important enough to house in a new location. Some items may be obvious, such as material that has become useless because of its age, or material on subjects no longer of prime interest to the organization served. In some cases, replacement of older bound journals with microfiche or CD-ROM versions may be feasible. Knowing in advance what will not be moved might well give the library time to find either a commercial buyer or a worthy recipient for the material.

Once the collection has been weeded, there should be a careful shelf-reading carried out. This simply helps ensure that books will be placed in correct order in the new location.

Determining quantities. The librarian should prepare statistics as accurately as possible concerning what amounts of each type of material will be moved, such as monographs, bound journals, loose material (e.g., patents, technical reports), and special items (e.g., films, videocassettes, microfiche collections). In terms of items needing special containers, it might suffice, for example, to record that 12 letter-size vertical files would be moved and placed in the technical report section of the new library, an exact count of the number of reports not being required in this case. But for books and journals destined to be housed in conventional shelving, it would be necessary to have a very accurate record of how many volumes of each would be moved. One reason for this is that the moving company must know this figure so as to estimate how many containers would be needed and, more importantly, to estimate roughly the number of work hours needed to move the collection. If some volumes must be given special treatment, such as rare books, this fact should be clearly stated. The requirements for such materials might affect the move considerably.

Location of materials. It is essential that the librarian carefully plan where the collection will be housed in the new library. The more detailed the instructions are for placement of materials, the less chance for mistakes. It is not enough to tell a mover to place boxes 10 through 12 on stack 19. A shelf should be selected for each container and marked clearly on the container to simplify the work of the movers. Color codes might be useful so that periodicals are marked with a green label and monographs with a red one, for example. This eliminates obvious mistakes in putting containers in the wrong stack areas. Before the move is made, it is essential that adhesive labels be placed on the new shelves to match the markings on the appropriate container(s). Labels should be held in place securely but should not be difficult to remove after the move. It is obvious that a representative of the moving company should completely understand the marking system.

If the new library will have enough space after the move so that the collection might appear rather small, outsiders might conclude that too much space was planned for the collection. To avoid this problem, it is wise to plan how the collection could be spaced out so that a casual observer would not feel the collection was too small for the space planned. One technique would be to leave the bottom shelves and the top shelves empty, saving them for future growth. This would have to be written into the instructions for the movers and not left to chance.

Preparation of shelving and materials. The new shelving should be cleaned of surface debris before the move begins. If possible, the collection to be moved should be cleaned if it is noticeably dirty. Special vacuum cleaners for book stacks might well be used in such a case.

Scheduling the move. The librarian must ascertain the degree of tolerance the organization served would have for disruption of service. In some cases all important services must be maintained during the move, even if this involves, for example, renting duplicate models of computers or word processors so that computer searching or report writing are not affected during the move. Other services, such as recording new journal issues, might well be exempt from special efforts to provide them during the move. Once the conditions of service to be maintained are known, the librarian must determine how to time the move so that service is kept as normal as possible. One way to do this is to schedule a move to start at the end of a work week, such as Friday night and continuing on Saturday and Sunday. The extra cost of such a schedule should be known in advance as it might cost more than a move made during regular working hours. The need for limiting disruption of service might well make even a costly moving schedule worthwhile in certain cases. A law firm in the middle of a major case in court would not worry much about costs if service could be maintained without serious interruptions. Obviously a move to a new location will disrupt things a certain amount no matter how carefully a move has been planned. Staff members have to get acquainted with their new quarters and new locations of materials, but service as a whole should not be drastically affected.

Supervision. A member of the library staff must be scheduled to supervise the move every hour that it goes on. It only takes an instant for the wrong container to be emptied and contents placed on the wrong shelf. Hours of work might be needed to rectify such a mistake. If the job goes on night and day, the librarian may have to use a lot of ingenuity in finding staff members for each hour. Perhaps compensatory time off may be permitted. This is a case where involvement of the staff, acting in a cooperative manner, would certainly pay off. All instructions should be typed and explained carefully to the supervisors well in advance of the move. Instructions for coffee breaks expected by the movers should be included, as well as breaks for meals. Needless friction could develop if a supervisor did not know when and for how long work would stop during breaks. Supervisors should be introduced to the moving company supervisors in advance, and both groups should see the new library before the move starts.

Emergencies. No matter how well planned a move may be, emergencies can arise, such as violent weather, strikes, lack of delivery of materials, or last-minute absences of personnel. The librarian should resolve not to become upset by any problem, keeping calm and making moves in a sensible matter. Conditions might cause postponement of the move. I have known of libraries where delays in the arrival and installation of shelving made a move impossible at the scheduled time. Any serious changes in schedules should be discussed by the librarian with his or her supervisor, but minor difficulties should be handled without referral. Violations of the contract for the move (should any occur) must be noted and discussed with the moving company supervisor at the time rather than risk the movers claiming they were not notified of a deficiency in time to remedy it.

Post-moving duties. Unless a move was extremely carefully carried out, it would be wise to plan a gradual shelf-reading project when time permits after the move. Even the best book movers can make mistakes when handling thousands of books.

Duties related to the move. Besides the duties mentioned above, there are several other responsibilities the library has that must be taken care of. These include notifying appropriate people and organizations of the new address and telephone number of the library, arranging for computer service during the move, etc.

The librarian of a prominent accounting firm in New York City prepared a very detailed schedule of such tasks for herself and her staff to follow, with the person responsible for each task clearly marked, along with a date when the task should be completed.[1] An adaptation of her schedule sheet is shown below—preparation of such a schedule is highly recommended for all libraries involved in a move.

Task	Person Responsible	Date Due
Order printing of address cards	FT	6 weeks ahead
Order new rubber stamps	LZ	7 weeks ahead
Print new library forms	FT	6 weeks ahead
Notify vendors of new address	AL	6 weeks ahead
Send address cards to libraries	FT	3 weeks ahead
Tag shelves-preliminary plan	EG, RT	3 weeks ahead
Tag shelves as planned	EG	1 week ahead
Tag furniture to be moved	AL	1 week ahead
Coordinate computer/phone moves	JJ	7 weeks ahead

Obviously no two libraries would use the same schedule, but those planning a move should do some investigation to be sure that the schedule will represent realistic deadlines, especially when one is dealing with telephone and computer equipment, usually so vital to the smooth operation of the library.

In conclusion, it should be apparent that moving a library is a complicated process, one which would benefit from careful planning. A text which covers all phases of planning and carrying out a move, written by Spyers-Duran, is well worth studying.[2]

REFERENCES

1. Personal communication from Janet How, librarian at Ernst & Whinney, New York, NY.

2. Spyers-Duran, Peter. *Moving library materials*. Rev. ed. Chicago: American Library Association; 1965. 63p.
A small but useful discussion of the problems of moving a library. The first section analyzes the major aspects of making a move, such as scheduling and labeling. The next section discusses the techniques of moving, including types of containers or trucks. A model contract is shown and described, along with sample specifications, in the last section.

PART II: ADVANCED ASPECTS OF PLANNING FACILITIES

Chapter 6

Pre-Planning Activities: What to Do Before the Architect Arrives

Deborah S. Panella

INTRODUCTION

By now you have probably completed many of the preliminary steps required to plan a special library. Before you proceed any further, look over your work. Have you based your plans on present conditions? If so, start over! In the early stages, you must keep in mind, first and foremost, that you (or your predecessor) are often to blame for at least some of the failures of your present library or information center. If you begin planning the new facility with preconceived notions, you will have set limits that do not necessarily exist. At least in the beginning, you should "think big." Allow your mind to wander into fantasy, to think "if only the library had

---

Deborah S. Panella is Chief Librarian at Paul, Weiss, Rifkind, Wharton & Garrison, 1285 Avenue of the Americas, New York, NY 10019.

...," and you will literally open up new doors. If you don't dream about what could be, you will wind up with what you already have. A wish list can, and will, be modified as planning progresses, but it is often impossible to expand space once you have stated your requirements. Set your sights high, and then prioritize your goals. Expect compromises. You will make them daily, but so will everyone else, so choose battles wisely. Know what you are willing to fight for and what you can live without.

A FEW PRELIMINARY STEPS

Don't be surprised. Take charge right from the start. Don't wait to be told you are about to move to prepare space and staff projections. Although you may not have formal plans, you should always have in mind at least a rough form of five-year growth plan. Better still is an annual report containing the library's objectives, even if no one else sees it. This will force you to focus on the library's purpose, review your accomplishments, and outline your hopes for improving operations in the future.

Read. In order to plan effectively, begin by reading at least a few books and articles about planning a library. Just by reviewing the bibliography in the back of this book, you will gain insight into the depth of planning and research required to do the job well. No one source will tell you all you need to know, particularly because there are so many varieties of information centers. Select a few articles and books that cover planning and space requirements generally, as well as those that cover your particular type of special library. Then select a few that concern libraries very different from your own. A handbook on public library buildings may be helpful in basic layout goals despite its different market orientation. Again, don't narrow your focus too early, or you may not benefit from the knowledge and experience of other types of librarian.

Gather internal information. As early as possible, try to gauge your company's time frame, obtain the actual or proposed location of the building, and determine whether a preliminary floor plan has already been discussed. This brief status report allows you to know where your planning participation is to begin, and how much time you have to prepare.

Find out which administrators or partners will spearhead the design committee and what style these influential people prefer. Most likely they have a few favorite office designs in mind already, and it can be very helpful to recognize their tastes. Similarly, if an architect or design firm has been selected, try to obtain a brief list of other libraries they have designed.

Your firm's position on the value and scope of the library will have a direct impact on the space you are granted. It helps to know up front whether your departmental design is conceptualized as a high-tech showcase or a stuffy room behind the scenes. If you suspect the worst, now is the time to focus on marketing the library as a vital information center in order to argue for more and better facilities.

Also try to assess the plans for the entire company. Get involved in the design at the company level, rather than just the library. Ask to be included in weekly or monthly planning sessions on design. Volunteer to do some research (phone surveys or literature searches, for example) to gain access to these meetings, or make a friend on the committee who will keep you posted on developments. Find out about company-wide automation plans, office sizes, and telephone systems. Working in isolation is not only lonely, but can also head you in the wrong direction. It probably won't work to fight for ten library PCs if your word processing department with double your staff will only get one. Conversely, if you request a 96-square-foot office, that's probably what you will end up with, even if employees at your level in other departments are assigned 150 square feet.

Now is also the time to gather information from your users. Patrons often have very good comments, and their perspective should not be forgotten. After all, serving their needs is your primary focus. Each organization is unique, and it may or may not be possible to send out a formal survey or personally interview everyone. Do survey at least a sample of your heaviest users, and have a suggestion box near the main exit. You should also contact a few nonusers now, to determine if there is any reason that the current space serves to keep them away. If you have a library newsletter or company-wide magazine or newsletter, it would be wise to solicit comments from those readers, too. If possible, it is a good idea to post preliminary floor plans in a visible spot, with a comment sheet nearby. Most people are curious and will take a few minutes to check out the plans, even if they did not respond to your survey. As you progress with plans, keep patrons informed, so that they are not surprised or disappointed with the final results.

Finally, don't overlook the value of your own staff. Remember, they are actually your in-house experts. Not only is it important to involve them for the practical point of view they provide, but it is also important to include them for the sake of morale. If you have ever felt decisions were made without consulting you, imagine how you would feel if your new work quarters were designed without your input. Staff members have a right to be consulted, and your space will be better planned if their advice is considered. Employees know best what is needed in the way of work space to perform their job. You do not do their tasks, and cannot know as well as they do what is necessary. As early as possible, begin talking to your staff individually and collectively, and continue to do so throughout the planning process. Depending upon the size and experience of your staff, you may have to do formal surveys or pry comments from people. In any case, keep people informed about the progress. If they know the design plans along the way, they will be much more confident and secure that they will like the new offices. You will encounter less resistance and fear from them on moving day.

Attend seminars. Most national and local library associations offer annual conferences and conventions, as well as occasional workshops and seminars. Although there are a few exceptions, most of the educational programs sponsored by the associations are excellent and cover a wide variety of topics. These conventions and conferences, while offering seminars and lectures, also provide an environment that serves as a gathering place to exchange ideas, policies, and practices. The same is usually true of seminars and workshops offered by library schools, independent consultants and private companies; so if there are seminars or conferences in your area, do try to attend. Again, even a session on law library design may help you plan a technical library. The overall goals and operations of these very different libraries are essentially the same, despite their specialized collections and clientele. Most of these seminars are conducted by consultants in library design or by librarians who recently survived a move. Those by consultants are particularly valuable, since the speakers have often planned a wide variety of information centers, with different budgets, automation, and space needs. You will leave a one-day seminar with a notebook full of good advice. They have seen architects who are terrific and those who can't tell a bookcase from a file cabinet, so they are full of wonderful anecdotes. And, frankly, if you haven't started laughing yet, you should do so soon or you will not survive the grueling months to come. Meeting other attendees also provides an opportunity to discuss strategies with librarians who are experiencing similar confusion and frustration.

Go to conference exhibits. It is important to keep up with new products and technology because it may have a significant impact on the design of your library or on your operations. An excellent way to learn about new developments is to spend time at the exhibit booths at major conferences. The sales and customer representatives are often eager to discuss the newest products as well as those still in the development stage. They are also looking for your reactions, so this is your chance to make suggestions. If you live in a major city, you will have several opportunities during the year to visit the exhibit booths of publishers and of furniture and supply, online service, office automation product, and personal computer vendors. Check local listings for trade shows and try to attend a variety. If you live far from a major city, you may be limited to viewing the exhibit hall at an annual out-of-town convention site, so do schedule plenty of time to go through it carefully. When you return to your office, contact vendors immediately for more information about the products which are of interest to you. Although they will eventually contact you, it is better to approach them at your convenience while the products are still fresh in your mind.

VISITING OTHER LIBRARIES – THE VITAL NEXT STEP

Although it is always an important part of any job, once you are in a position of authority and responsibility, it becomes essential that you keep in contact with colleagues in a formal and informal way. One of the best times to contact your friends in other information centers is prior to planning your new facility. Seeing how other libraries operate is an excellent way to broaden your horizons and unleash your creativity. By visiting other libraries and information centers you will gain insight into their design strengths and weaknesses. Because each library is unique in its operations and environment, there is much to be learned by visiting a few. Undoubtedly, the entire facility will not match the needs of your company, but certain features may suit your organization perfectly. Therefore, it is important to keep an open mind when you select libraries to visit and when you actually go on tours.

Whom Should You Visit?

The optimum number of libraries you should visit depends in part on your previous work experience and the number of libraries you have visited informally in the past. However, five to ten libraries seems an appropriate number for most of us. Go to other libraries and information centers that are both similar and different in size and collection. Plan to visit law firm, bank, corporate, science, medical, or technical libraries. Do not limit yourself to your type of library, or you will have set limits to your imagination.

Although it is wonderful to see state-of-the-art libraries, it is also important to see libraries that are smaller and less sophisticated than what you hope to have. It may sound like a waste of time to tour such small, antiquated facilities, but there is often something to be said for the creativity of cramped librarians and the value of some old-fashioned methods of doing things. Just because you are planning new space doesn't mean you won't be faced with insufficient space, either immediately or in a few years. One of the first communications from management is likely to be a statement that you won't get all you ask for, so it is wise to be prepared to deal with too little space.

Another destination should be at least one library or information center designed by the architectural firm selected by your company. Seeing a finished product of the firm with whom you will be working is an excellent way to determine how well they understand library goals and operations. Furthermore, the librarian there may have some helpful hints on how to communicate with the architects to get your desired results. If it is not possible to see other libraries that the designers have completed, contact the librarian(s) by phone or mail for their help. Even from a distance, you should be able to gauge the attention the library received during the design phase. If you find that the architectural firm selected has never designed a library, put together a neat package of carefully selected and organized material for them to keep as a reference. The architects will see that you have done your homework and may appreciate that you are providing them with information too.

Several of the libraries you visit should be in fields quite different from your own. Because they are different in the size or scope of the collection does not mean that you have nothing in common. The trip will still be very helpful. For example, you may see a unique method for shelving or storage of newspapers, or a great arrangement for maintaining vertical files. You may see a routing procedure or reference request form that could be modified slightly to fit your own needs. The library may have a new CD-ROM set-up you've been wondering about, or a microform reader-printer you've been considering. The important concept to remember is not to categorize your library into a field or type until you have examined all your choices. Do not start out with limits to your options and your operations or you will set restrictions in your design that come from ignorance or prematurely stereotyping your library.

When Should You Visit?

As soon as you begin to be involved in planning your new library, you should arrange to see a few libraries. This will help you conceptualize your needs and will give you a chance to see what options you may have. The first library you visit should be one of those designed by the architect your company has selected, so you can view problems and advantages firsthand. After you have seen two or three libraries, though, try to take a week or so to assess what you have seen before continuing your tours.

If you have seen a library that you think is especially well-designed and appointed, it is wise to try to return to it with your office administrator or design committee member and the architect. Doing the tour together is a perfect time to point out exactly what you like and dislike about the facilities and organization. Seeing your design goal in an operating information center may help them understand your priorities and viewpoint. If they can't or won't visit, try to draw floor plans and get the names of vendors, designers, and specifications for features you want to obtain or duplicate.

Plan to see only one or two libraries in a day, and keep visits between one and two hours. Longer visits are not appreciated by your guide, and you become burdened with too many details. If you need to return or call for additional information, do so, but keep in mind that your colleagues have their own jobs to do.

What Should You Look for When You Visit?

You may wish to take along a checklist or survey so you will remember to ask certain questions (see the sample checklist that follows). Some people even recommend taking along a camera to photograph particularly good examples of work stations, chairs, or design features. You should definitely take a tape measure with you, but ask the librarians if they mind your checking a few measurements before using it. Most people don't remember the shelf depth, the aisle width, and so on, and will be grateful that you are prepared.

Although it is difficult, attempt to put yourself in various roles as you tour each library. See the library from the eyes of a patron or client. What does the library do to make the person feel welcome and comfortable? How visible are the librarians? In what ways does the library turn you off? Is collection layout logical and easy to use? Are there adequate study carrels and work tables? Remember that the library is there for patrons' use.

Next, look at the library from a page's point of view. Library clerks and shelvers put in a long day in the library, and their space needs should be recognized as important. If there is a reading room at one end and all the shelves are at the other, the amount of walking done by the pages will tire and frustrate them, and you may need more people. If you haven't considered this in your staff projections, you will be short on space for the new person, starting a vicious circle. If you do not anticipate and meet staff needs, you may find yourself recruiting shortly after you move into the new facility.

Now view the library as your home. After all, you spend almost 2000 hours a year here. How happy are you with the creature comforts? Is there a water fountain nearby? Where are rest rooms? Is your office private enough that you could fire someone there? Are there any places for you or your staff to relax? Should you have a staff refrigerator or microwave oven?

Finally, imagine the process of ordering a book, receiving it, cataloging it, shelving it, and signing it out. Does the layout of the library help or hinder the processes and procedures that make up your days? If the work flow is hampered by the design of the library, are there ways that the problems could have been avoided?

Be certain you consider the placement of the library in relation to other departments. How far is the firm's mailroom? Since the library receives a high proportion of the firm's incoming mail, it is important to be easily accessible to the mailroom and freight elevators. Also note the location of reception areas and conference rooms, since you will need to decide whether you want company visitors wandering into the library.

Does the library use off-site or basement storage? If so, what is kept there and how often do they use it? How is it maintained? It may make more sense to store material in another building if the rent is lower, the material is rarely used, or the space within your building is unacceptable. For example, if the books you want to retain are rare and valuable, it may be preferable to store them off-site than to store them in the damp, musty basement of your building.

This is a good time to compare your library services to those of your colleagues. Although this sounds like a different mission, you should also look at the types of services being offered by the libraries you visit. Are they offering services you don't? If so, have you made a conscious decision not to provide them, or were you restricted by space and lack of staff? With more space in the future, should you expand the library's role in your organization? For example, clipping services; checking conflicts; maintaining internal memos, briefs, and files are projects under the direction of the librarian in some law firms.

Take a good look at the appearance of the library staff. Are they dressed in suits, or are they more casually dressed? Do they present a professional image? How do they answer the phones? How do they talk to their patrons and each other? Is there chatting or laughing, or are they too busy to catch their breath? How does your library staff compare? What image do you want to present? Since many changes will be taking place at the time of the move, you may wish to redefine your dress code and work ethic at the same time.

In summary, keep your eyes and ears open for every detail of your visit, and you will be certain to get the most from it. As mentioned earlier, there is something to learn from information centers of every size and variety.

Some Rules of Etiquette

Limit your visits to two hours or less, and plan no more than two library tours in a day. If you are tired, you will miss important details. Furthermore, it is likely that you will run late if you schedule too much for one day, and your host will not appreciate your late arrival. If you are going to be delayed or must cancel, please call. If you plan to have other librarians or design people with you, make sure the librarian knows who the guests will be in advance.

Be complimentary during the tour, but be sincere. "I love your wastebaskets" is a bit ludicrous. If you can't find anything nice to say about the space or layout, you can probably feel good about saying "You are a genius to accomplish so much with such limited space." Although people don't usually mind being asked what they would have done differently if they could do it over now, you should not be the one to suggest the errors.

If you have many questions, you should invite your guide to lunch at your expense on another day to discuss the library operation and layout in more detail. Your visit should be a pleasant interchange between two professionals, not a question-and-answer session.

Accept the answers to your questions graciously, and do not press when none is given. "I don't know" is a perfectly acceptable answer in this situation. Remember that this person is already doing you a favor and should not be asked to compile information for you.

Nor should you ask for technical help with calculations of shelf space, staff needs, or anything else. You can ask what formula, if any, was used, but don't expect anyone else to do your work.

After the Tour

After you return to your office, take stock of what you have seen. Make notes if you didn't already, and then call or send a nice note of thanks, with a few nice comments about the library. If the tour guide was exceptionally helpful, you might even consider sending a basket of fruit or a box of candy.

Based on your visits to other libraries and other early preparation, you should be ready to begin actual design of your own facility. If time permits, now is the time to write a report covering the goals and objectives of your library, how you hope to improve future operations, the role technology will play in the design and operation of your information center, and space and staff projections. This document should be as carefully written and documented as possible and should contain current and future needs, with calculations presented in a readable and logical manner. In a meeting, you will not be able to remember the details you have collected without your personal library design reference book.

The more knowledgeable and confident you are in the initial contact with the architects and administrators, the more respected and trusted you will be. Without your input, the library design will no doubt suffer, and without their support you will have a difficult time gaining control of the library design.

A Sample Checklist

Library_____ Librarian_____
Date of visit_____ Number of staff_____
Square feet_____ Number of patrons_____
Linear feet_____ Number of patron seats_____
Size of collection_____ Year library completed_____
Architectural firm_____
Moving company_____

Shelving

Vendor_____
Metal or wood?_____
Shelf height_____
Shelf depth_____
Shelf unit width_____
What percent is empty?_____
Range length_____
Reference shelves?_____
Compact shelving?_____
Floor load_____
Aisle width_____
Are shelves braced?_____

Seating

Carrels or tables?_____
Dimensions per person_____
Surface material (i.e., wood, veneer, formica; light or dark)_____

Chairs (i.e., wood or padded, with coasters or not, firm back or reclining_____

Location of patron phones___

General Design

What formula, if any, did the librarian use to predict shelf growth?
_____
How many offices are there for staff?_____ Size?_____
Is the library on interior or exterior space?_____
   If exterior, what is adjacent to windows?_____
   Are there blinds or curtains?_____
How many colors used?_____
Lighting (fluorescent, recessed or dropped, candles, etc.)_____

Placement of light switches and outlets_____
Signage (plastic, bronze, silver, paper)_____
Excessive? Inadequate? Clear? Friendly?_____

Special Comments

_____
_____
_____
_____
_____
_____

Chapter 7

Planning:
A Cooperative Effort

Arleen N. Somerville

Libraries and information centers of today require extensive and flexible electronic capabilities, in addition to the capability of fulfilling traditional functions such as housing collections and providing reader space. Effective planning for such libraries requires an understanding of users' needs and use patterns, involves all affected staff in planning, and utilizes skills and knowledge of other library staff as well as staff from other departments of the organization. Development and maintenance of rapport between library planners and architects and the organization's planning and engineering staff is crucial. The best results occur when library planners and other participants demonstrate respect for each other's perspectives and priorities and thus are able to negotiate compromises.

LIBRARY PLANNERS

Responsibility for coordinating the planning process should be assigned to specific staff. In a small facility, the director may assume that role. In a larger library, it may be more effective to delegate planning to the library's facilities planners or to staff members in the relevant unit.

Selection of a primary library planner is pivotal, for that person should be able to coordinate discussion among the planning com

---

Arleen N. Somerville is Head, Science and Engineering Libraries, University of Rochester, Rochester, NY 14627.

mittee and represent library needs in an informed, assertive, and tactful way. The planner is the primary contact with the overall building coordinator, consultants, architects, facilities planners, interior designers, and other organization staff external to the library. The planner must ensure that open communication is maintained among these groups, library administrators, and library staff. The relationship of the planner and other library staff to planning committee members is a key factor in achieving a successful design. The staff and planner must devote considerable effort to developing credibility with the building coordinators, architects and engineers. One way to achieve this is for the primary planner to ensure that reports and data are provided at meetings and as needed, as well as to participate actively in completion of the building program document.

The primary library planner may opt to share responsibilities with other librarians in the unit. Advantages of this approach include: utilizing the skills and knowledge of other librarians, reducing work load of the primary planner, and providing professional growth opportunities. For example, one librarian can become the millwork expert and another the electrical and telecommunications or lighting specialist. In all cases the library planners must quickly become knowledgeable about designing new buildings. This education process is necessary, even when library consultants are available.

Early responsibilities of library planners include estimating new space needs for the collection, service areas, readers, and staff. Institution plans, technological changes, and budget levels affect growth rate calculations, as well as the decision to build a facility of a particular size. Often several general plans that project different overall space needs may need to be developed before a specific square footage figure is decided upon.

Planning activities continue from the initial alternative space proposals through detailed decisions about service areas, shelving, seating, equipment, electrical and telecommunication systems, lighting, furnishing, staff offices and workrooms, colors, fabrics, and signage. The final step is planning the move.

Developing and maintaining open communication, completing reports, gathering data, and attending meetings requires much time and effort over several years. When library staff who plan new or renovate old facilities take on this task in addition to other full-time responsibilities, it is extremely difficult to juggle and complete all aspects of planning to the optimum level as well as carry out normal responsibilities.

If the library director is not the primary planner, it is essential to keep him or her up-to-date on progress. The director may participate on or chair the planning committee. The prestige and authority of the director can help achieve significant building improvements for the library. Some of the director's possible responsibilities might be delegated to or shared with an assistant or associate director.

Planning Committee

A planning committee helps to bring together individuals from the wide variety of groups involved in a new building or renovation project. The committee's membership may change over time, as planning and construction progress. The committee chair might be the library director (or designate), the building construction coordinator, or the primary library planner.

An initial planning committee might include a consultant, library administrators and planners, institution planners, and possibly architects. Once the project is underway, a planning committee is needed to ensure open communication lines, provide a forum for discussing building-related topics, keep participants informed about building progress, and provide an opportunity to discuss change orders. This group should then add the institution building coordinator, architects (project, design, and technical), institution engineers and facilities planners, field representative, interior designers, and consultants. Sometimes representative users are included. Minutes should be kept and distributed to all participants. If these minutes are not kept by a library planner, they should be monitored closely to ensure accuracy, because they become the basis for action or interaction. Frequency of meetings may vary, depending on need.

EXTERNAL BUILDING PLANNERS

Consultants

Consultants may be librarians with planning expertise or architects who specialize in libraries. Consultants' expertise can be used in a variety of ways. It is advisable to bring in consultants as early in the process as possible. The initial plans for the new facility prior to fundraising can benefit from outside consultation. Once the decision is made to proceed with detailed design and construction, it is wise to utilize the expertise of a consultant.

Consultants are valuable links between librarians and architects and are useful for most projects. They are especially valuable if either librarians or architects have had little experience planning research libraries. Even when the participants have had some library planning experience, consultants provide in-depth knowledge that infrequent library planners may lack, serve as informed advocates for the library to the architects and the institution planners, and help avoid major mistakes that are difficult or impossible to remedy later. Consultants can help analyze library operations and space needs, help achieve optimum locational relationship between functions, and assist in preparing the building program. Consultants who know which architectural features are negotiable and which are not can be especially helpful in the negotiations necessary to achieve a balance between aesthetic concepts and function.

Consultants may be retained only to complete interior design, or the same consultants may work on the entire project. Specialists in library interior design bring expertise that in-house designers may not have.

Architects

Challenges of working with architects have been described by Robert Rohlf in his article about common pitfalls encountered in planning new libraries.[1] Few architects have designed libraries, especially research and special libraries, therefore most lack an understanding of functions in those libraries. Direct contact of library planners with the architects is absolutely essential to achieve a functional and esthetic design.

It is crucial to inform architects about space needs before the esthetic concept is established in their minds. Once this concept is set, basic changes are unlikely to be achieved. The architects must be given extensive information about the library, often in a short space of time.

Providing them with written reports, involving them in discussions, facilitating their observations of staff and user activities, and sponsoring their visits to other libraries are ways to expand their knowledge. Some important general guidelines for architects about library configuration include the following: rectangular or square spaces are best, because this permits the greatest amount of flexibility; each floor should be as large as possible to limit the number of floors; each floor should be as open as possible to provide flexibility; floors should be contiguous.

A description of staff activities has two purposes: it defines functions of each area, and it defines the optimal location relationships between areas, based on how the functions relate to each other. For most functions there are staff and user needs. Areas whose functions are important to describe include, for example: reference desk and other information activities; reserve reading (how does it differ from reference activities?); workroom activities; end-user searching areas; security requirements (i.e., allowing only one entrance/exit, and including all stairways within the security system); confidential areas; and current journal display. Use patterns and information needs of users that affect design are important to mention, also. For example, users frequently consult recent journal issues so that area should be close to the entrance.

It is essential to establish and maintain an effective working relationship with the architectural team throughout the design phase. It is important to support the esthetic ideas of the architects, while also stressing the functional needs of each area. Negotiation is usually needed to achieve a balance between esthetics and function. Being open to new ideas from the architects can produce exciting results. Discussion of architects' proposals may require tactful but firm responses when changes in their designs are necessary. Architects vary in their reactions to such discussion, from those who readily adjust design to meet functional requirements to those who are extremely defensive and resist design changes. In the latter case, consultants and the library director can often help achieve crucial changes. Mutual respect and credibility are achieved more easily if the library planners are prepared for meetings with data, questions, and comments. Architects are more likely to ask questions if responses are prompt. Throughout the process, a sense of humor will help planners survive challenges. It is essential that accurate minutes be kept of the meetings with architects, because they are used for reference and to inform architects who join the design group at various stages of the process. The minutes will document changes throughout the design and construction stages. Even with good communication some agreed-upon changes may not be made and others not agreed on may be incorporated. It is essential to review each new version of design, millwork, lighting, power, equipment, and furnishings blueprints to ensure that they show plans and changes as agreed upon.

Including architects on site visits to other libraries can be extremely beneficial. The architect can see good and bad design firsthand. The planners' credibility is enhanced when other librarians repeat the same design preferences and objections. Encouraging architects to participate actively in the discussions increases the value of the trips.

Sometimes library planners work with a series of architects, with the project manager, and design architects involved from the beginning. The planning details may be completed by one of these architects or by another architect who joins the group at a later point. Technical details, such as lighting, power, and heating/air conditioning are planned by an architect with special expertise, who generally joins the planning team further on in the process. Each time other architects join the activity they should be briefed on previous discussions, decisions, and your priorities. If major design difficulties develop after the design architect is no longer a regular participant in the planning committee, it is best to discuss these directly with him or her, rather than working solely with the architect who completes the planning details.

Field Representative

A field representative may be appointed by the architectural firm or the organization. This representative's job is to coordinate activities between the architects, construction crews, and the institution's engineers. Developing an effective working relationship with the field representative is crucial for several reasons. He can serve as an advocate for library needs and suggest checking a question with library planners. The field representative can alert library planners to problems that might not otherwise be brought to their attention and can provide accurate information about construction progress.

USERS

Because the library is designed to serve the needs of the clientele, it is important that library planners understand their users' needs and use patterns.

Astute library staff regularly monitor such needs and use patterns. However, special efforts to solicit ideas from users early in the planning process will add to the understanding of clientele needs and bring them into the communication process in an active way. Retaining support of users during renovation or new building construction is easier when active communication lines are maintained. User groups vary by institution. In academic, government, and industrial organizations, users include professional, research staff, and faculty, while academic institutions also include undergraduate and often graduate students.

Some institutions include representative users on the planning committee. If this option is not followed, group meetings of representatives from each user group can be productive. These groups can be defined as appropriate in each organization. Often, frequent library users are included, but infrequent users may bring new perspectives to the discussion. In academic settings, student groups benefit from viewpoints of frequent users, leaders of student professional societies, and student library workers. A separate discussion group for students permits them to express themselves without constraint from faculty. The wording of the invitation to participate in all discussion groups should set the tone for encouraging all comments and ideas, as well as outlining the general topics for discussion. During the meeting the leader may schedule an initial brainstorming time so participants can propose ideas without evaluative or judgmental comments. One way to begin this discussion is to ask attendees to indicate their top concerns. During the second part of the meeting these ideas and others can be discussed and analyzed. The leader and other library staff should keep questions and comments neutral to avoid influencing the discussion.

Discussion topics may vary by organization. Typical topics might include: alternatives for organizing the collection; relationship of different parts of the collection to each other; seating preferences for different functions and with different parts of the collection; shelving location of microforms in relation to printed materials; ways to control noise, if that is a problem; uses and arrangement of microcomputers; access after regular hours, if relevant; space-saving options; security issues; and lighting.

While users will draw on their own library experiences, it may be helpful to provide attendees with background information so they can discuss the issues in a more informed context. This information may be general, such as amount of space available and probable functions in the new area. Or the information could be more specific, such as listing possible organizations of the collection along with positive and negative implications of each, or describing compact shelving. Notes of the meeting should be distributed to attendees as a way of maintaining communication.

If quantifiable data is needed, a written survey may be the answer. Only crucial questions should be selected, so the survey is not too long. Background information can be provided to encourage more realistic response. The wording of the questions should facilitate the collecting of useful data, but at the same time be easy to answer and compile. A check-off method that asks users to select a number from 1 to 5 with cross-checking questions, may work well. Space should also be left for general comments.

It is wise to review planning progress with representative users. These discussions can provide valuable suggestions and keep communication channels open.

LIBRARY COMMUNITY

Library Staff in Units

It is important to involve all staff who will work in the new facility, for staff will accept and welcome change when they have an opportunity to participate in discussions and decisions. Better planning decisions are made when staff have an opportunity to convey their knowledge of the functions they perform. Maintaining communication with staff throughout the planning process facilitates their acceptance of change and incorporation of their ideas into the plans.

Early in the process it is crucial for library planners, in conjunction with the staff, to identify in writing the various functional areas and describe the activities in each area. This document serves as an overall review for all staff, especially if the unit's new organization will differ from the past, and can be used during discussions with architects and interior designers. Functional areas include, for example: the circulation desk, reserve reading desk (in academia), information/reference desk, workroom, offices, end-user training, end-user searching of external and internal databases, other microcomputer areas, and photocopiers. At this point an initial list of equipment and furnishings needed in each of these areas can be developed. Future functions should be identified, such as telefacsimile transmission of documents and computer acquisition and check-in of journals. Planners, along with other staff, should describe the preferred location relationships between areas, such as between circulation desk and information desk, information desk and professional offices, workroom and professional offices, information desk and end-user searching areas, information desk and abstracts, information desk and reference collection, information desk and online catalog terminals, workroom and delivery areas, bound journals and current journals, bound journals and abstract journals, and copiers and bound journals and current journals.

Other Library Staff in Same Organization

It is important to involve library staff from other units if there are any not affected by the renovation or new building to plan for library-wide implications and to utilize their expertise. The computer and systems staff should participate in discussions of such matters as cabling pathways, size and types of wires and cables, equipment placement and space requirements, and lighting near CRT screens.

Discussions with staff from circulation, reserves, reference, and microcomputer areas can determine what works well for them and what problems they have had. These staff, too, have experienced the impact of computers in their areas and can provide comments on electronic equipment experiences as well as on traditional matters.

Other Librarians and Libraries

Literature searches can identify helpful articles and books about traditional and electronic library functions. Until very recently, most computerized searches located information about traditional topics, rather than anticipating and meeting future electronics needs. Each December issue of *Library Journal* lists recently completed construction projects and those underway.

Workshops and conference programs are useful in learning how to incorporate newer technologies into library facilities and to identify resource people.[2] Such resource persons include consultants, equipment and furnishings sales representatives, lighting and ergonomic specialists, and other librarians with planning experience. Discussions with fellow librarians can be accomplished at meetings, over the phone, or on visits to their libraries.

Visits to other libraries can be most helpful. Librarians are remarkably willing to discuss examples of poor design and ostensibly good designs that don't function, as well as positive design features of their libraries. This is an excellent way to accumulate ideas about end-user facilities, microcomputers and other equipment, electrical and telecommunication requirements, information desks, circulation desks, signage, lighting, and overall space usage. Participation of architects in these visits is beneficial and should be encouraged.

INTERNAL BUILDING PLANNERS

Building Construction Coordinator

The organization will generally appoint a building construction coordinator, usually a physical facilities department head, to oversee the entire project. This coordinator may delegate considerable responsibilities to others or participate actively at the operational level. The coordinator may chair planning committee meetings or attend meetings, except when highly detailed work is discussed. In all cases it is important to maintain a good working relationship with the coordinator, so he or she will be more likely to advocate library needs. If coordinators make it clear that they value informed responses from librarians, others on the construction and engineering staff will also ask questions of them. This is important because when questions arise it is easier and faster not to consult. This lack of consultation can lead to disastrous decisions that may impair the effective functioning of the library.

Telecommunication Staff

The extensive, growing, and changeable telecommunication needs of the electronic library should be discussed with staff from the organization's telecommunication group, the engineers, and the architects. These discussions should also include library computer staff and of course, library planners. A description of power needs of computerized catalog, circulation, and processing systems is useful. In addition, access to data lines into the organization's computer systems, access to external telecommunication networks, and local area networks should be considered. Other microcomputer requirements for the library that should be explored include CD-ROM, text and graphics data processing, spread sheets, and use of files via central-switching apparatus or a mainframe. The importance of achieving flexibility for future needs should be stressed. This variety of electronic requirements and the need for flexibility necessitate conduits large enough to add future cables and wires (both to the building and within), raceways and rack-mounted power strips to carry wires, and convenient locations to pull wires from raceways to equipment that will change over time.

Engineering Staff

The organization's engineering staff work closely with the architects, construction contractors and subcontractors, and facilities planners. Therefore, it is important that library planners maintain open communication channels with their engineering staff in order to gain their support for changes in building plans, help the planners stay posted on progress and problems during construction, and encourage the engineers to ask questions rather than to make their own decisions.

Facilities Planning

Many organizations include a facilities planning department whose staff are responsible for coordinating and designing renovation of existing facilities. This work usually extends to new buildings also. Close and open communications with these staff are crucial to successful planning. These staff become aware of questions raised and problems experienced by engineers and construction crews and can bring questions to library planners. They can also be important advocates for the library.

Interior Design

Interior design work may be the responsibility of the facilities planning group or another in-house unit, the architectural firm, or a consultant. An advantage of having an in-house group handling the design work is that these staff may have worked on enough other building projects to know what the needs of the organization are. Their approach is also most likely to be least expensive. The architects who designed the building should possess a solid understanding of the functions and priorities of each area, based on earlier discussions and design work. An outside consultant may have experience with library interior design and, after acquiring an understanding of the local library needs, can achieve an attractive design.

CONCLUSION

Major factors in achieving successful library design hinge on the library planners' abilities to coordinate and work effectively with the wide diversity of fellow team members: the organization planning coordinator; organization engineering, facilities, and telecommunication staff; architects; and consultants. Such efforts require that library planners maintain constant and effective communication with everyone. Library planners who are informed, assertive, and tactful are more likely to be successful in this challenging, frustrating, and exhilarating experience.

REFERENCES

1. Rohlf, Robert H. Library design: what not to do. *American Libraries.* 17(2):100-104; 1986 February.
2. The Building and Equipment Section of the Library Administration and Management Association, American Library Association, sponsors a Library Facilities Planning Discussion Group at each ALA Annual Conference and Mid-Year Meeting.

Chapter 8

The Role of the Architect in Library Planning

Robert R. Thrun

The role of the architect in library planning is to provide the librarian and the library's users with an environment that meets their needs and functions. The role of the librarian is to provide the architect with the information he or she needs to design a pleasant, humane, and productive work environment.

Architectural design is a cooperative process of discovery. Think of library planning as a hierarchical, highly logical decision-making process where earlier decisions imply later ones, where broad concepts become more defined as the planning process evolves. It is a process that begins with qualitative information and becomes progressively more quantitative.

Architectural planning consists of six separate phases. The first two phases, programming and conceptual design, may be performed by the architect who is designing the library or by another firm. The four base services—schematic design, design development, contract documents and construction administration—will be performed by your architect (see Figure 1). What these phases are and what occurs at each phase of a library's development will be discussed in this chapter.

PROGRAMMING: DEFINING THE PROJECT'S SCOPE

The librarian's first working meeting with the architect or architectural team marks the beginning of facilities programming. Pro-

---

Mr. Thrun is Principal Designer at the architectural firm CUH 2A, 600 Alexander Road, CN-5240, Princeton, NJ 08543.

68

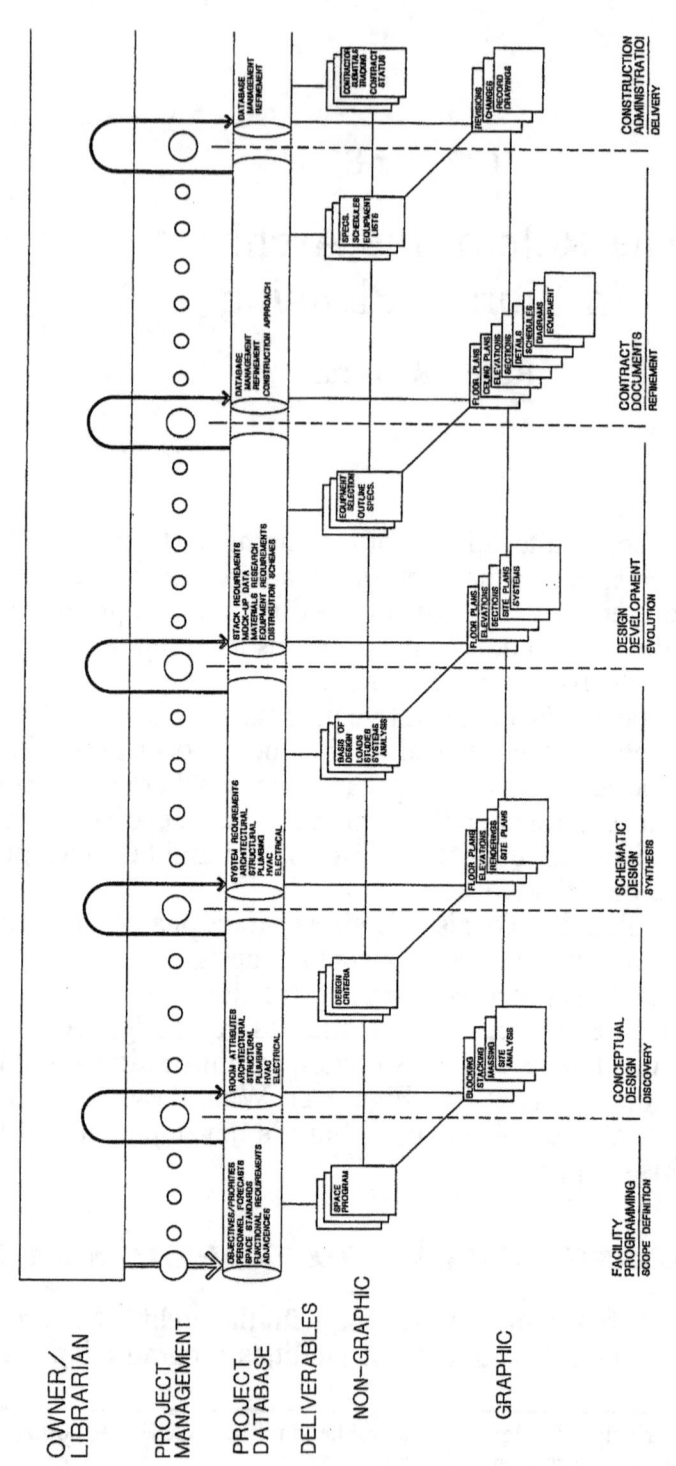

FIGURE 8.1

gramming is an information gathering phase, based primarily on interviews with librarians, staff, and users, to determine important factors that will guide the development of the library's design. During programming, the architect attempts to develop an understanding of the users' needs, of the culture and image of the workplace, and of the library's role within the institution or company.

The information provided by the librarian and gained from the architect's interviews becomes the basis of a project database that will grow and be refined throughout the design process. This database, which becomes more detailed and quantitative as the process moves forward — is a written and graphic description or definition of the library. In large facilities today, the complete database is often maintained on a computer-aided design and drafting (CADD) system.

Facilities programming determines the scope of the project. The information sought by the architect consists of the following types:

Objectives and priorities. The objectives and priorities of the librarian and the institution of which the library is a part determine what the library will be, more than any other factor. Much of the information sought at this early stage can be classified as behavioral. The architect needs to develop an understanding of the corporate culture, of attitudes toward the library. Is it, for example a place where research is conducted by individuals or by groups or is it merely an information warehouse? Does the current library achieve its objectives, or was it designed for a purpose that no longer suits the institution's needs? Does corporate policy or attitudes toward the library concur with the librarian's own ideas?

This is an area where the librarian's thoughts and preferences will be most critical to the success of the library project. We encourage librarians to think carefully about what they would like their library to accomplish at this stage of planning. The information will be very subjective, and may be nothing more than a sense of what the library should be, but it will guide the entire development of the space. The ideas developed here will shape the concept of the library.

Also helpful to the designer are the librarian's and corporation's preferences. If you have been favorably impressed with another facility, or with the way a particular problem or function has been handled at another library, that information will be useful to the designer. Although every library is unique, ideas that have worked well in one facility may be adapted to another.

These are broad questions, but they are essential to help the architect discover the character of the institution in order to design a library space that is compatible with that character.

Personnel forecasts. The architect must plan for the library's future growth, and the more detailed and long-range the librarian's forecast can be, the better. Two areas must be considered: growth in the library's staff and growth in the number and type of library users.

Space standards. Most larger corporations and institutions have space standards that determine both the amount and type of space provided for a given job classification. A department director, for example, may be allotted 150 square feet in an enclosed office. A manager may be allotted 100 square feet in an open office workstation. Other job functions will have varying space allotments in varying environments, depending on their functional needs. Space standards are normally established by the facilities manager in a corporation, institution, or a large library. Existing space standards will be reviewed and incorporated into the plan. If no standards exist, they will be developed based on preferences, budget, and functional needs.

Functional requirements. At a very subjective level, the architect needs the librarian and corporate management to answer the question, "What is the function of the library?" Does the library, or company, or institution view the library as a strictly utilitarian place where materials are housed and research is conducted by staff professionals? Or is the library a place where people are encouraged to browse through shelves or review current periodicals or informally discuss ideas with their peers?

At a more utilitarian level, the architect needs to know what functions need to be housed in the library. For example, if the library is for reference only, a circulation desk will not be needed, but substantial space will be required for on-site research. If a major objective is to encourage greater usage of the library and greater interaction of a research facility's staff in the library, then a large and inviting public area may need to be designed. If computers are to be in the library, the architect will need to know who will use them—staff, patrons or both—and how it is anticipated that they will be used. Computers and other forms of equipment have very specific electrical, lighting, and mechanical systems requirements that must be incorporated into planning.

Adjacencies. This asks the question, "Where does it make the most sense to locate the library within the institution?" The library's ideal location will depend on the library's objectives. If the library is intended only as an information source for laboratory researchers in a specific department, a location near the laboratories may be preferred. If the library is intended to encourage interaction among professionals from varying fields within the institution, a location near the main entrance or other high-traffic public functions will be more logical. If the library is intended to be a public statement of the corporation's commitment to research, a highly public location will be preferred.

Through this examination of requirements, the architect will begin to define a sense of space that will define the library and help to reinforce the library's goals as an institution. A broad sense of design requirements will begin to develop. Based on the needs of various users, intended uses for the space, and current and future equipment and space requirements, the architect will develop the space program for review by the librarian and corporate management.

The written programming document defines the scope of the architectural project. It is a highly qualitative document that commits to paper the architect's findings from the preliminary information-gathering process. It will not contain any specific answers, but it will begin to suggest the size and location of the library.

The programming document will be reviewed with the librarian and other members of the project team. After approval, the architect begins the second phase of the process, conceptual design.

CONCEPTUAL DESIGN: DISCOVERY

The facilities program defined in the broadest sense what the library should do. Conceptual design explores the options available to achieve the program's objectives.

Still operating at a highly conceptual level and in very general terms, the architect begins to explore the ramifications of what was learned in the programming phase on the available site or sites. The special library is usually part of a larger project, a space within a larger space. In conceptual design, the relationship of the entire project to the site and the relationship of functional spaces within the project are examined.

An additional layer of information will be gathered for each of the functional spaces within the building, and the concept of the building and of the library will be further defined. Using the objectives and priorities, personnel forecasts, space standards, functional requirements and adjacencies for each space as a starting point, the architect and project team will determine generally the architectural, structural, plumbing, HVAC, and electrical attributes of each room or function.

As yet, these spaces are unrelated. We know what functions the library must house. We know what departments or functions the library should be located near. We know what support systems the library will require. But the library is still one piece of a puzzle that remains to be assembled. After this information-gathering process, the architect produces two sets of information for the project staff and librarian to review: graphic information in the form of blocking, stacking, massing and site analysis diagrams and a written report of design criteria.

The graphic information is a group of conceptualizations that help to determine how and where the project should be located on the site, what its basic form should be, and how the interior functional spaces could relate to one another to accomplish their objectives, from floor to floor and within the space of each floor. All of the major forces acting on the project, e.g., site restraints, accommodation of adjacency requirements within and through floors, corporate and library objectives, are graphically represented. The architect's exploration of various means of achieving the objectives stated in the space program will be represented in these diagrams. Typically, one stands out above all others as the best balance between accommodating the institution's needs and its budget.

The second product of conceptual design is a written statement of design criteria, which is a refinement of the space program that incorporates the room or functional attributes that were determined, as well as support system requirements.

Taken all together, the information gained and analyzed will indicate a size for the library and requirements for its location. Conceptual design will not necessarily specify a location, but it will suggest and lead to one.

SCHEMATIC DESIGN: SYNTHESIS

The schematic design phase is an extension and refinement of programming and conceptual design, where the priorities that were established and the decisions that were made during these phases are translated into a basic plan of the library space. It is the beginning of actual design. The first decision to be made is the location of the library within the building. In programming, we determined the basic requirements for location of the library. In conceptual design we stated the functional or room attributes of the building: architectural, structural, plumbing, HVAC, and electrical. In schematic design, the library begins to take physical shape as the architect and librarian determine the exact location and square footage of the library.

There are two types of products of schematic design: graphic representations of the building and its spaces in the form of floor plans, elevations, renderings, site plans and modules and a written document called the basis of design. The basis of design is an engineering-oriented document that includes analyses of structural loads and supporting (mechanical and electrical) systems requirements.

The graphic materials will begin to define the building with some specificity. All rooms and spaces of the building will be drawn to scale, each labeled with its appropriate function. Typical configurations will be indicated. Locations of the library entrance and exit, areas where windows and daylighting could be exploited, locations and approximate sizes for workrooms, offices, stacks, and other functional areas of the library can all be defined for the librarian's consideration at this point, and options can be explored. Within functional areas, plans will indicate placement of partitions, furnishings, fixtures and layouts.

Computer-aided design and drafting (CADD) can greatly assist here and in design development. CADD replaces time-consuming and expensive manual drafting efforts with computer-generated images based on project data that is stored in a database. This information can be easily manipulated to produce variations of floor plans that allow the librarian to examine all possibilities.

The materials delivered to the librarian in schematic design provide a fairly accurate description of the library. When the librarian and architect approve the schematics, they will have reached an agreement on what the library will be. In design development, the next phase, this agreed upon design is refined.

DESIGN DEVELOPMENT: EVOLUTION OF THE LIBRARY SPACE

In design development, the librarian frequently works with both the architect and interior designer as final detailed plans are developed that include exact locations of walls, furniture, equipment and facilities required by the program. Design development actually represents the completion of approximately 35 percent of the working drawings for the library. In this stage, the architect prepares plans, elevations, sections, and other supporting drawings in detail.

In addition to thoroughly defining spaces and furniture during design development, planning is done to accommodate the equipment the library will have at the move-in date, such as microform readers and printers, computers and copiers, as well as equipment that will be needed in the future.

Planning for the future is very important in developing libraries because of the rapidly changing nature of library needs. Change implies cost. If future changes can be planned and accommodated during the initial design of the library, they can be integrated logically into the library at the appropriate time with minimal disruption and cost.

Replacing or supplementing card catalogs with computer terminals, for example, is a change that has major impact on supporting systems. Although space requirements may be the same or reduced, new and expensive issues are raised. There are no electrical requirements for a card catalog; computer terminals have substantial electrical requirements. Lighting requirements for people using card catalogs are fairly typical of the paper-and-pencil office environment. Lighting requirements for the user of a video display terminal are very different.

With exact spaces and their functions defined, the architect, interior designer and librarian will define the detailed functional characteristics of the furniture and equipment planned for the library. What type of study carrels should be used and what should they contain? What type of desk should be provided for library users? The answers to these types of detailed questions will provide a further basis for the selection and specification of furniture and equipment that furthers the objectives of the library and meets the needs of staff and users.

During design development, the architectural team and the librarian will also begin to discuss and define appropriate types of finishes for walls, floors, and ceilings. Materials will not be specified at this stage, but they will be defined generically. The floor covering, for example, may be defined as carpet tiles of a particular grade because they meet requirements of cost, maintenance, noise reduction, ease of replacement, and ability to withstand high foot traffic as well as the wear caused by wheeled book carts.

Specific decisions about lighting requirements for various areas of the library and differing tasks to be performed there will also be made, with the librarian providing input on functional requirements and the architectural team using its technical expertise to meet those needs.

By the end of design development, all fixed elements, such as walls, windows, and partitions, and all impacting elements or engineering systems, such as electrical, HVAC, and plumbing, have been defined. In addition, the materials to be used in the library — carpet or other floor coverings, wall coverings, ceiling materials — will have been defined generically. Types and quantities of furniture and equipment will also be known, and the interior designer may have presented an overall palette for the librarian's consideration.

The written products presented to the librarian and project manager at the conclusion of design development include outline specifications of all equipment and systems planned for the library. The graphic products are the floor plans, elevations, sections, and other drawings. If the library is part of a larger building, the information of most concern to the librarian will be the floor plans and written specifications. Other materials related to the building may be shown to the librarian for informational purposes. Together these documents provide a complete picture of the library, with only exact finishes, exact furniture and exact specifications for lighting and equipment to be determined.

CONTRACT DOCUMENTS

The architectural decision-making process ends for the librarian when design development is complete and the project enters the contract documents stage. Fixed and impacting elements have been determined, and the architect will prepare the drawings and specifications required to bid the project. A large portion of the interior design process still remains. Types of finishes and furniture have been selected, but they still need to be specified. This topic will be covered in more detail in Chapter 10.

The contract document stage is a refinement of design development. During this phase, the architect prepares final drawings for submission to contractors and determines the staging of the construction project. Specifications, schedules, and equipment lists are prepared in final, detailed form. Together these written and graphic materials describe the work to be performed, the responsibilities of the different parties involved in construction, and the conditions under which the work is to be done. These materials are reviewed by the librarian and project manager before entering the construction administration phase.

CONSTRUCTION ADMINISTRATION

Once the architect has prepared, and the librarian and library or building project team have reviewed the contract documents, the contract documents serve as the basis for contractors' bids. From this point on, selection of the contractor or contractors and most of the day-to-day work and supervision of the project will be done by the company's or institution's project manager with assistance and support from the architect.

During construction, most of the librarian's attention will be focused on preparations for the move into the new facility. Interior plans will be completed with the interior designer. A signage system should be developed with the graphic designer. Furniture and equipment will be specified and ordered. The existing library's collections, as well as any furniture and equipment that will be relocated to the new library, will be prepared for the move.

As a final point: Although all of the architectural planning was completed in the design development phase, a few decisions will probably have to be made during construction. Changes and problems are inevitable during any construction project, and some rethinking may be required. This is a cooperative effort that involves the librarian, the project manager and the architect.

A FEW WORDS ABOUT BUDGETS

The size of the budget is only one of several factors that affect the design of the library. It is helpful to keep that in mind during the early phases of design. Every librarian who is planning a library probably has a sense of what the budget will be or what corporate or institutional standards will allow. Let that be a guide, but do not let it rule out the accommodation of needs or wishes that you feel may be too expensive.

The librarian should approach the planning process with a sensible wish list. Items or features that appear to be expensive might actually be incorporated into the plan inexpensively. Items that are expensive but add great value to the library as a corporate place or a work environment may actually take priority over other features that are not as important or that can be accomplished less expensively. The architect is a problem solver, who will attempt to accommodate as many needs and desires as possible within the budget.

The architectural process contains a number of checkpoints where decisions can be made on what to incorporate and at what cost. It is best not to make these decisions before the process begins. It only shortchanges everyone.

Budgets will be reviewed by management at the completion of each stage of the design process. This is done routinely to assure that the design process stays on track and that program objectives are being achieved. These budget reviews allow needed changes to be made incrementally.

A SUMMARY OF DELIVERABLES

At each phase of the library's design, graphic and written materials will be presented to the librarian and project staff for review, discussion, and approval. A summary of the basic materials provided during each phase follows:

Pre-design services. Pre-design services include the programming and conceptual design phases. As mentioned earlier, these necessary phases are not considered part of the basic architectural services. Consequently, they may be performed by the architect or by another firm or consultant. The completed program should outline all net and gross spaces, required special equipment, desired characteristics of the space, and a statement of goals.

Schematic design. At the conclusion of schematic design, the librarian will be presented with full schematic design documents showing locations of all planned partitions, small-scale furniture and equipment layouts, and major defined spaces. If the library is a separate building, the librarian will also be provided with sections and elevations, along with sketches, perspective sketches, and models to convey the basis of the design. If the library is part of a larger building, the librarian may be shown these materials for informational purposes, but no decisions will have to be made. In addition, written and graphic materials to provide preliminary analyses of mechanical and electrical systems and equipment will be provided.

Design development. Plans, sections, elevations, and sketches will be provided as necessary to show final partitions, furniture, and equipment layouts. Outline specifications that describe the final architectural and engineering materials and equipment will also be delivered.

Contract documents. Final plans, elevations, sections, and detail drawings that set forth the requirements for construction will be delivered. Final specifications for architectural, mechanical, electrical, structural, and other engineering services required for the library will be presented.

Bidding and negotiation. At this point, if the library is part of a larger building, most of the construction-related work will be handled by others within the company. The architect prepares bidding lists, documentation of bidding results, analyses of bid alternates, and final contract documents.

Construction administration. The architect delivers shop drawing approvals, change orders, and project cost accounting documentation.

Chapter 9

Estimation of Shelving Needs: Selection of Equipment

Tony Stankus
Kevin Rosseel

ESTIMATING CURRENT HOLDINGS IN LIGHT OF FUTURE NEEDS

While it is a fool who does not order all the shelving that could possibly fit, some sort of justification for specific amounts is generally demanded by architects and purchasing directors. Managers want to know how much you have, how fast it grows, and sometimes if any weeding can be done. How fast it grows is probably the most critical statistic the librarian must provide. Assuming that the library has been in existence for sufficient time, an examination of perhaps the last five years' records can, as will be shortly seen, give a workable projection. Librarians for entirely new libraries must guess, projecting from their current budget and experiences of sympathetic colleagues. Whether any weeding can be done is partly under the control of the librarian. Most librarians are likely to be reading this chapter because their best efforts at weeding have not succeeded in delaying the need for a new or expanded library.

About the only statistics, then, that can be reliably ventured are

---

Mr. Stankus is Science Librarian, Science Library, Swords Hall 100, College of the Holy Cross, 1 College Street, Worcester, MA 01610. Mr. Rosseel was his Assistant, and is currently at the Indiana University Graduate School of Library and Information Science.

Illustrations by Mark Shea. Mr. Shea is a commercial artist, and Assistant in Serials at Holy Cross's Dinand Library.

the current volume count and the amount of shelving this has come to occupy over time.

There are four common methods for estimating current holdings:

1. *Direct count.* This method involves sample tallying of what is on the shelves. This method is appropriate when the collection is largely books and bound periodicals as opposed to files and soft-bound reports. A motivated clerk can count one thousand volumes every twenty minutes. The tedium can be relieved by breaking up the periods devoted to counting.
2. *Sampling from shelves or case.* This method usually involves taking a random sample of isolated individual shelves and bookcases and doing an actual count of what these contain. If your sample of shelves or bookcases is not markedly biased, you get a good approximation by multiplying the sample by the total shelves or cases.
3. *Estimating from catalog card files or other records.* If the collection is fairly uniform in size (most items falling within a certain common thickness and height range), then holdings and space requirements can be measured from card files. Catalog cards typically measure one hundred cards to the inch. Surprisingly, even on a hard computer disk holdings can be measured by polling the number of unused spaces, a routine matter. Subtract to get occupied spaces. Estimate the number of spaces per document or book to get the total.
4. *Relying on published estimates of volumes per shelf or case.* With very large collections, it is easier to count shelves or whole cases and use published volumes per shelf on case standards. These can be found for law, medicine, etc.

The volume count is then considered in the light of the number of your shelves or cases occupied. You estimate the time over which this space-filling has occurred to get a growth rate per year, with some added weight perhaps, for more recent years. It is then a short, if somewhat uncertain step, to venture your minimum added shelving requirements for as many years of growth and floor space as the architects and financial officials will allow.

FIXED METAL SHELVING
FOR BOOKS AND BOUND PERIODICALS

Metal library shelving is of two basic designs: two-post and four-post. Two-post is by far the most common for most library applications. See Figure 9.1A and B. In most schemes a rectangular frame whose external dimensions are usually 36 inches wide and from 72 to 90 inches high is bolted to a base. The base provides some stability and can also serve as the bottom shelf in some versions. Less often, the frame might be bolted to full-length supporting side-panels. (Side panels are most often decorative, however.) In either case, the posts are usually slotted on opposite sides at intervals of about half an inch to provide for the convenient installation of clip-on shelves and their height adjustment. There is a designed flexibility in whether a shelving unit will be made single-faced or double-faced. Most single-faced metal shelving units can be turned double-faced by simply extending the base on the opposite side and clipping on shelves above it. Single-faced units usually have to be bolted flush to walls with clips that are attached near the top of the unit. Double-faced units dominate most stacks areas in long lines of parallel rows. Typically, these units are braced perpendicularly across the tops of the aisles with metal bars. This doesn't interfere with aisle traffic unless your clientele are basketball players.

Selection of individual shelf depth is related to both the internal bracing of each unit and the size of the typical volumes to be stored. Most twin-post library shelving today has rigid rectangular frames with welded joints. This arrangement prevents swaying of an upright unit from side to side. But some older versions rely on X turnbuckles, a criss-cross bracing system at the back of the bookcase. This does the trick with only occasional need for turnbuckle retightening, but does limit the depth to which a book can be slid back on the shelf. This is an important point, since one is generally paying for the space beyond the end of the metal shelf! It works this way: The typical double-faced unit will have about a two-inch post. See Figure 9.2A. Assume that you attach at the same level two seven-inch shelves on opposite sides of the post. In the absence of cross-bracing barriers or a backstop, you get a shelving surface straight through of sixteen inches (fourteen inches of metal surfaces

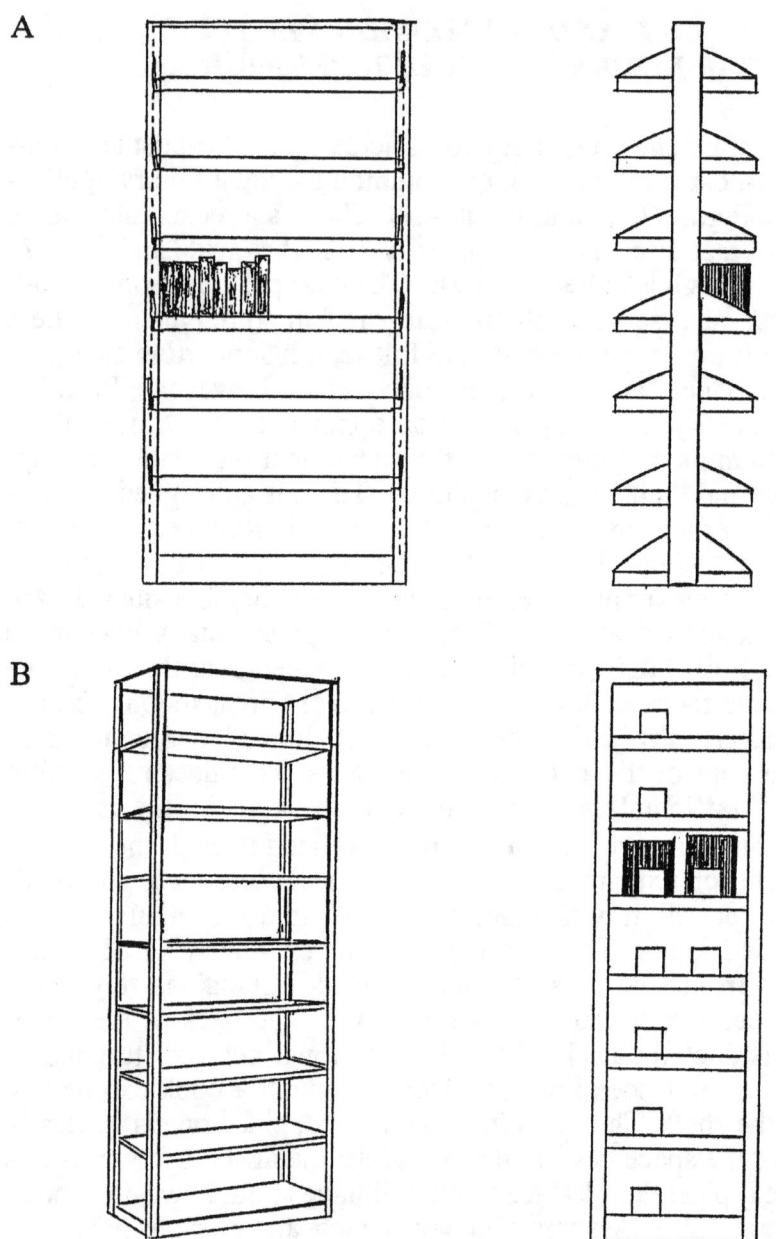

FIGURE 9.1A and B. Comparing two forms of shelving. Figure 9.1A depicts a 2-post unit, by far the most common in most stack areas. The 4-post unit in Figure 9.1B is still in use in some storage applications.

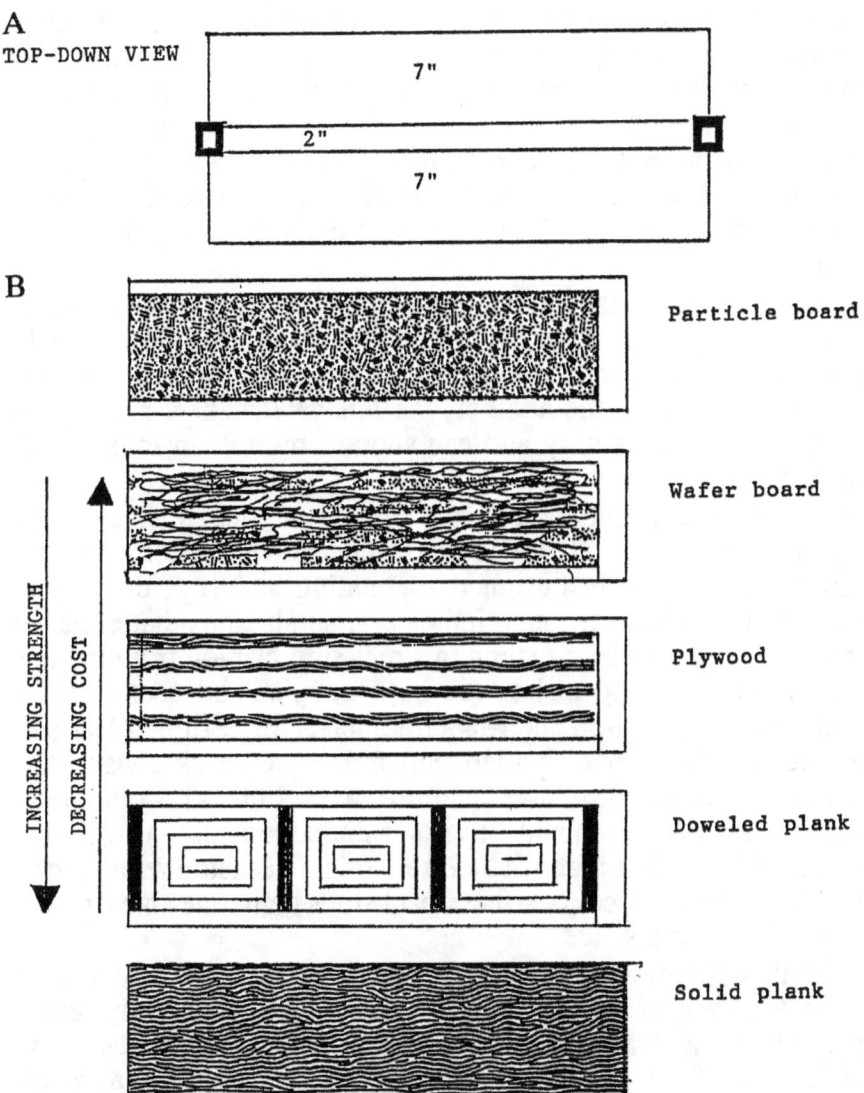

FIGURE 9.2A and B. A illustrates the "nominal" shelf measuring system of some suppliers. They might argue that the arrangement in B, with its two 7-inch shelves separated by a 2-inch gap, amounts to giving you two 8-inch shelves. Be careful in your specifications to indicate exactly how much metal pan you actually expect. B shows the interior composition of some popular types of wooden shelving today. Generally, over time, the more expensive plank types bear more weight with less sag.

with a two-inch gap in the middle). It is not uncommon for manufacturers to tell you that you are getting eight-inch "nominal" or "virtual" shelves and to charge you for them. As a practical matter, indicate clearly that you wish eight-, nine-, or even ten-inch actual shelves, depending on the horizontal extension of your titles. Some overhang on the interior side of the shelving is tolerable, but an outward projection of spines leaves them open to damage from aisle traffic.

One other source of specification confusion is the thickness of the metal shelving. Given the same material and form, thicker metal shelves can support more weight. Thickness is typically expressed in gauge. The lower the number, the *thicker* the sheet metal. Sixteen-gauge is quite sturdy and can support more than thinner, 22-gauge metal.

Two-post metal shelving offers a number of convenience and appearance options. Wood or woodgrain side panels are common and, although not primarily designed for adding stability, do provide some. Aisle markers or range indicators, small signs that either lie flat against end panels or extend in street-sign fashion from the tops of the bookcases into aisles, are both popular and useful. Some companies offer clip-on shelf-label holders. Some firms offer special shelves that can be pulled outward to serve as consultation counters. Libraries with large quantities of softbound, floppy technical documents or annual reports should consider using some shelves with dividers that can be inserted in a backstop with notches every inch or so. Of course, these backstops deny one an extra inch or two of shelving space.

Probably the most significant option is whether to buy a metal canopy top for bookcases. While they are far less commonly seen in general-purpose libraries today, they offer two conveniences in special libraries. First, they provide a measure of protection from ceiling leaks or fire sprinkler discharges, no small matter in a laboratory or industrial building. Second, they allow the attachment of overhead aisle lights that can be turned on and off as needed. Wiring is easily run through the hollow components of posts. Of course a canopy does restrict the spacing of shelves below and the allowable height of books placed on top shelves.

Four-post shelving is far more commonly used for the storage of boxed documents or the flat shelving of atlas-sized materials than for shelving regular materials. Many four-posters lack the metal end panels for each shelf found in all two-post systems. Nonetheless, four-posters offer some advantages (see Figure 9.1B). Virtually all four-post shelving has a fairly sturdy enclosed base and a canopy provided at no extra cost. Four-post shelving is often available in much greater shelving depths than two-post shelving, and there is no confusion over whether or not the air space found in double-faced shelving is useful or assessed against you in the billing, since it is all real metal shelf. Much four-post shelving, however, gives the distinct impression of industrial warehousing, and fewer of the amenities sold for two-post shelving are widely available.

WOOD SHELVING FOR BOOKS AND BOUND PERIODICALS

Wooden shelving today comes in a very wide range of finishes with oak, walnut, and birch the most common. The veneer typically covers the top, bottom, and front edges of the shelving. There are basically four types of interior composition (see Figure 9.2B). Arranged in increasing order of strength and cost, they are: particle board (granular wood by-products glued together), wafer board (shavings glued together), plywood (continuous thin sheets glued together), and plank shelves (usually several rod-like sections fitted together along their longest side, but occasionally a single, solid piece of wood).

The principal faults of particle board, and to a lesser degree waferboard, are a tendency to sag, and, should the veneer be broken, a tendency to crumble, particularly where the board presses on shelf supports. Single-plank boards can warp in humid surroundings: humidity is better resisted by doweled plank boards whose individual grains tend not to allow warping in unison.

The strength and stability of wooden bookcases depends on the sturdiness of the end panels and the fastness of their connections with both case and canopy. Some single-faced units have a solid back panel that limits shelving depth but helps the case to resist sway. With some wooden shelving, the back-to-back effect is achieved by having side panels and shelves that are 16 to 18 inches deep but have no back panel. Books can then be shelved from either side.

METAL OR WOOD SHELVING FOR CURRENT PERIODICALS

Loose issues of periodicals are usually shelved apart from both bound periodicals and books, often on slanting display shelves. This is partly to encourage current browsing and partly because the materials are typically softbound, floppy, and generally unable to physically stand unsupported. The first policy decision is the degree to which display value triumphs over storage efficiency.

The most common display-shelving scheme involves five or six hinged slanting display shelves (see Figure 9.3A). Four or five loose issues can be put out per display shelf. Underneath is a flat storage area, usually 4 to 8 inches high and nearly 36 inches wide. Although lacking storage efficiency, you get about twenty titles very attractively displayed for every 3 square feet of single-faced current periodical display.

The opposite tack involves laying the journals flat on shelves and merely labelling the shelves (see Figure 9.3B). Shelves can be layered every 4 to 8 inches, depending on journal thickness and the frequency of binding. Some metal shelves are slotted to allow thin, metal vertical dividers. These go a long way to maintain order in large collections. It is not inconceivable to efficiently store, and nominally display 28 to 40 journals per 3 square feet of floor space.

METAL OR WOOD SHELVING FOR REFERENCE AND INDEXING-ABSTRACTING AREAS

Reference-book shelving is typically larger and often custom made in wood owing to its decorative and functional prominence in the library. Three types of shelving arrangements are common.

The first is essentially a more generous version of the standard bookcase with a deeper shelf and a taller intershelf allotment (see Figure 9.4A). This typically reduces the number of shelves from six or seven to five or six but allows for the extra tip-out space required for the frequent and rapid removal of taller and broader titles with-

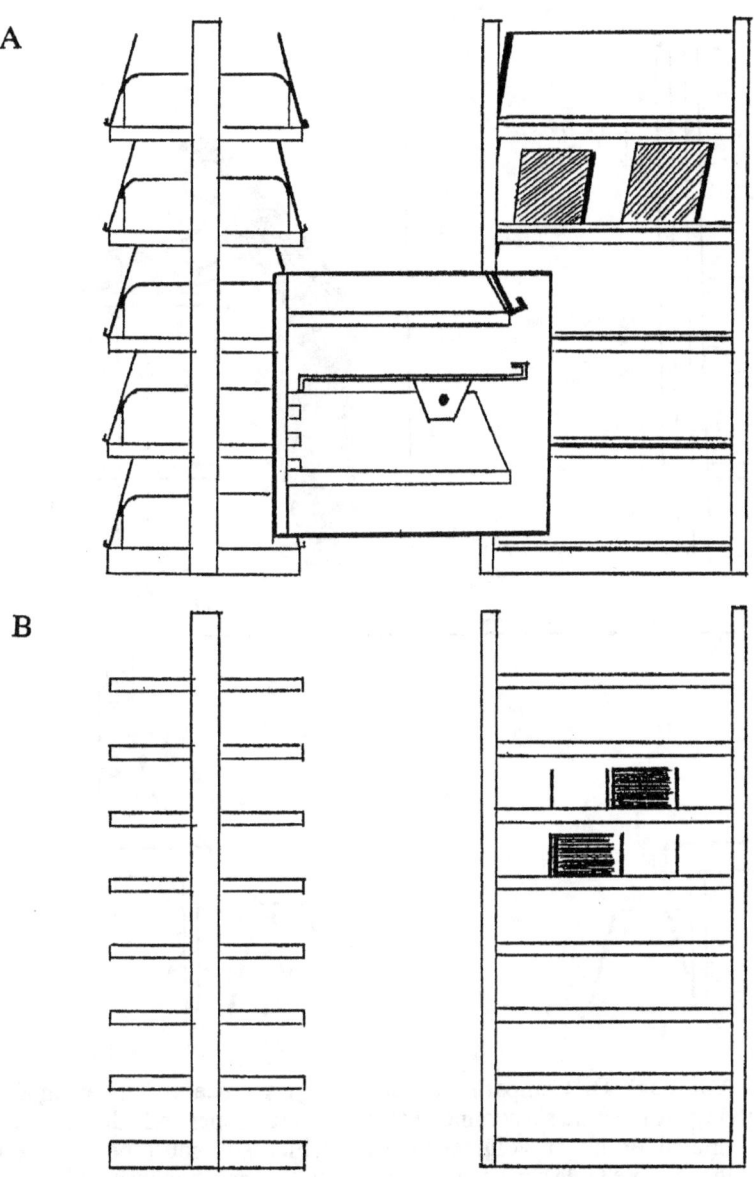

FIGURE 9.3A and B. Contrasting two of the more popular shelving schemes for display of loose, current journals. A, the hinged, slanting display shelf, offers greater esthetic appeal, but B, a flat shelving scheme, generally can house more titles in the same floor space. Dividers are generally available for flat shelving schemes to maintain order among stacks of loose issues.

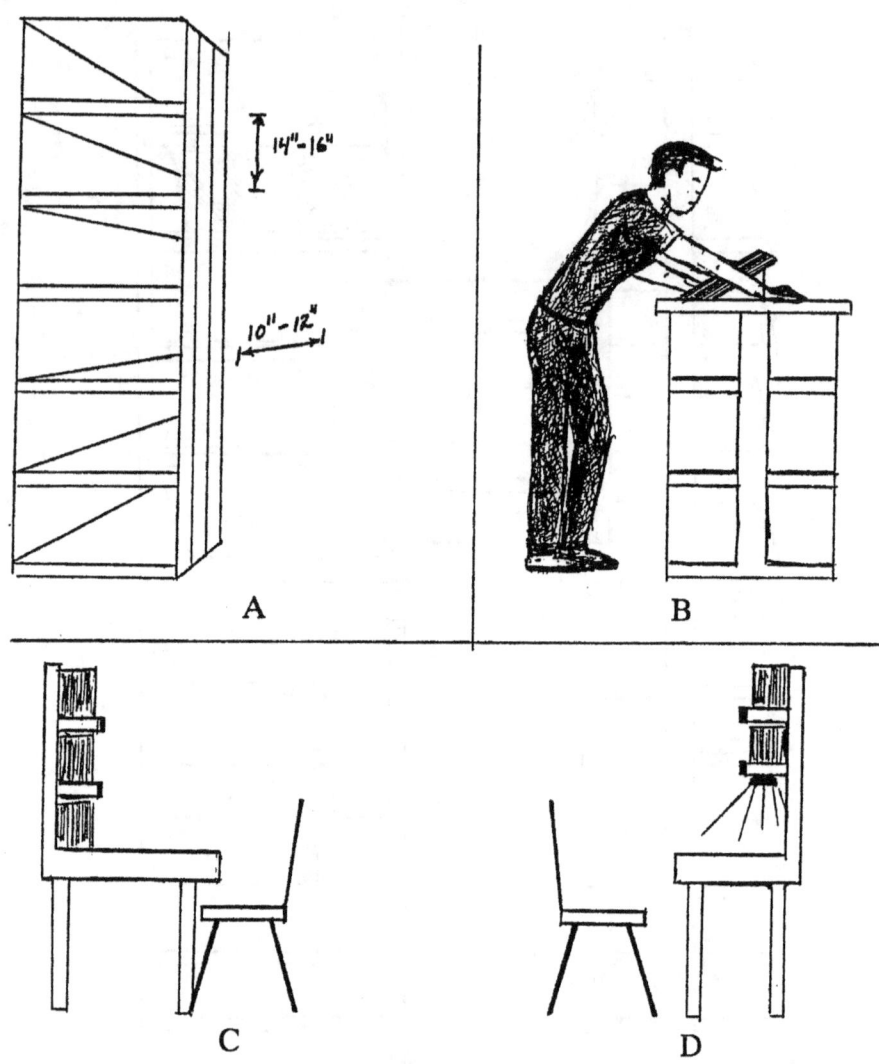

FIGURE 9.4A through D. Comparing schemes for reference and indexing/abstracting shelving. A illustrates a common scheme where deeper and taller shelves allow easy removal of larger volumes; needed tables still must be provided nearby. B provides some table surface in a countertop to a half-bookcase. C and D represent a strong emphasis on convenient table space and seating, at the expense of some shelving capacity. C provides three shelves, but takes up three extra square feet and depends on ceiling lights. D provides only two shelves, but is more compact and offers excellent light for reading the fine print of some reference or indexing works.

out snagging their top edges or corners. Typically, reference shelving has 10- to 12-inch deep shelves with clearances of 14 to 16 inches, as opposed to 7- to 9-inch deep shelves with clearances of 10 to 12 inches. But a hidden cost for this scheme of shelving is that you must still provide seating and table space nearby.

A second approach to reference shelving directly attacks the need for seating by incorporating the shelves right on desks or carrels. While the convenience is great for any one customer, there can be a problem of inconveniencing simultaneous users. Shelving efficiency is poor. One good scheme can either involve three shelves, the first of which is the desk's own surface (see Figure 9.4C). In this case the desktop should be about 3 feet deep. Another scheme has only 2 shelves, both of which are raised above the working surface. The desktop can then be 2 feet deep. A light underneath the lower shelf avoids shadows and aids fine-print reading (see Figure 9.4D). A relatively efficient three-shelf scheme houses approximately 45 volumes with seating in 13.5 square feet. A two-shelf scheme with a reading area underneath the overhanging shelves houses about 30 volumes in 10.5 square feet, including space for the seat.

A final approach to reference shelving that has some applicability to short-term indexing-abstracting searching provides shelving and consulting and note-taking space, but no seating. There are typically three reference shelves (half of a typical bookcase) capped by a finished wooden shelf that serves as a work surface. Most of these units are back-to-back so that a 2- by 3-foot countertop results. Assuming 3-foot aisles on either side of such an arrangement, you house about 90 volumes in 35 square feet (see Figure 9.4B).

There are a number of combinations of shelving and seating schemes. One can improve the lower storage capacity of the carrel-station shelving style by alternating it spatially with the shelving-only type of units shown in Figure 9.4A. It is common to have the most recent volumes on the carrel shelves with older years on shelving-only units behind the sitter, so that he or she might turn around and reach without having to relocate. One can alternate the consultation counter-type stations of Figure 9.4B with Figure 9.4A units. The lack of work space of Figure 9.4A units would be offset by their superior shelving capacity.

ROLLING COMPACT STORAGE METAL SHELVING

One of the slowest shelving technologies to take root despite enormous promise in floor space savings is rolling shelving. The technology is at least 30 years old. X-ray departments, law offices, auto spare-parts supply houses, and pharmacies have long been using it. The straightforward quality of the hardware and correct levelling at installation are far more important than any high-tech sensors built into some of the electrically powered versions. The units consist of conventional rows of shelving that glide on tracks in a special, usually raised, base. The heights and depths of the shelving tend to be very similar to fixed metal shelving: often some of the same hardware components are used (see Figure 9.5). The differences among various types of rolling shelving involve the source of locomotive power. In some lightweight filing situations where only 3-foot deep installations are involved, the librarian can supply virtually all the power. She or he uses a fixed handle to tug the unit along the track. Far more common is mechanical-assist shelving. Here there is a bicycle-chain-type gearing system hidden by end panels and extending to the floor. This system allows easy movement of loaded 6- to 12-foot-long ranges. The librarian can, with very little effort, turn a crank or ship-wheel at the end of each case to create an aisle in front of the desired bookcase. For facilities with truly heavy files (such as x-ray films), or for ranges of 15 feet or longer, an electrically-powered system is preferable. Here motors the size of a loaf of bread are mounted in the undercarriage beneath the shelving. A push-button on the end panel activates the glide. Surprisingly, each ton of books quietly progresses until the desired aisle is opened.

There are, of course, reasons why this form of shelving is not more common. First, while it can easily save you its cost in extra floor space construction, the notion of a unit that costs several times its equivalent in conventional fixed shelving still seems frightening. Second, while most ground or basement floors are probably strong enough and level enough to handle this shelving, above-ground floors usually require some structural reinforcement, and an engineering professional should be consulted in almost any case. Third

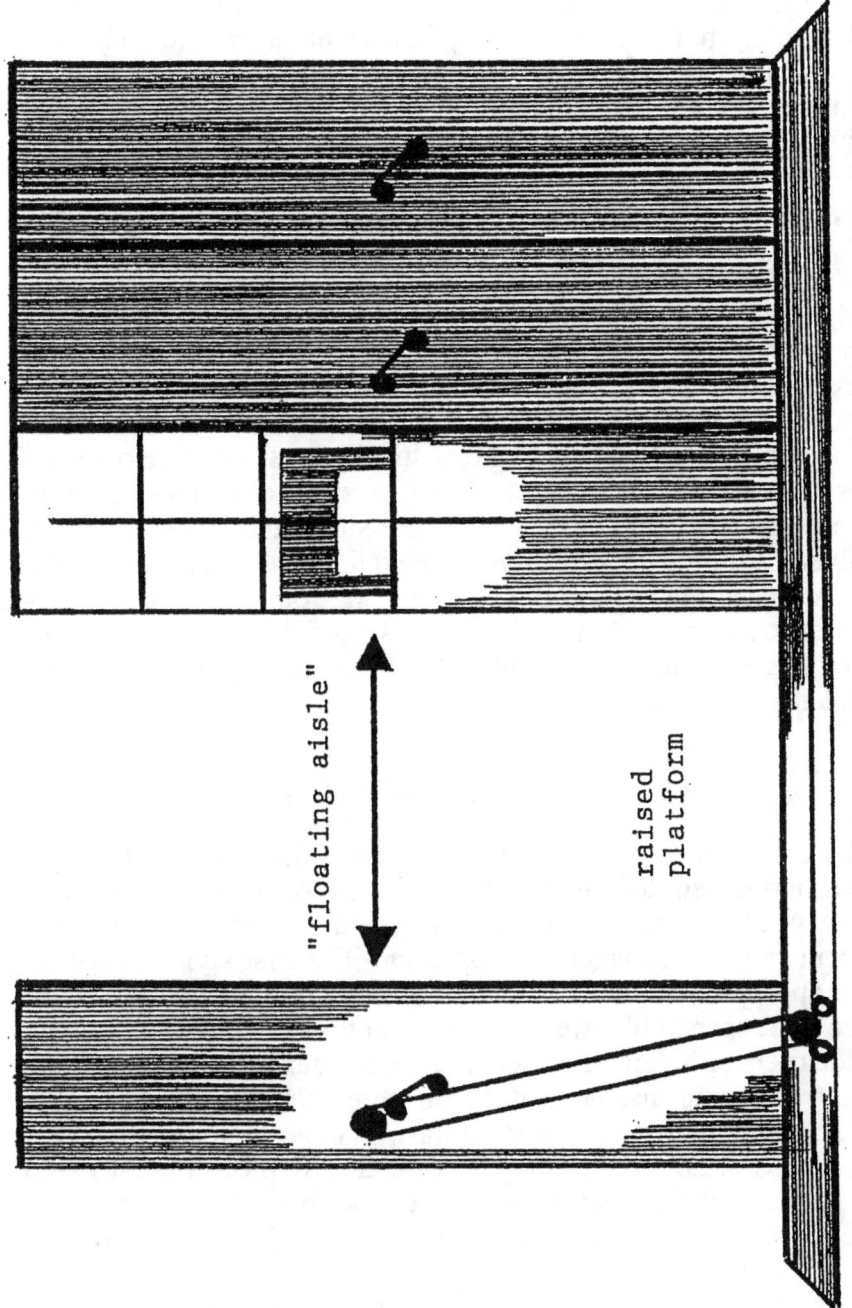

FIGURE 9.5. Rolling compact storage shelving offers enormous space savings by eliminating multiple fixed aisles. By turning a crank or activating an electric motor, heavy cases glide by, opening to the section you select. Most units are mounted on raised platforms that contain gear works or motors.

is the largely unwarranted fear of having patrons or staff crushed or otherwise injured. This is virtually impossible in simple manual or mechanical-assist types (they move too slowly and can be stopped by any reasonably firm object in the aisle) and is an extremely unlikely but possible occurrence in motorized units if all safety systems fail. Fourth are occasional but real problems: broken hardware, track-jumping, and unwanted drifting. The item of hardware most likely to break appears to be the chain. The repair is fairly simple. The side panel is removed, the flooring of the carriage is lifted, and the mechanism is restrung. The other repairs are not so simple. They usually involve some crow bar labor, and the billings can reflect this. (Surprisingly, there is rarely any off-loading of the collection during these repairs.)

Nonetheless, rolling shelving realistically presents more opportunities than liabilities. Where maximum storage deserves priority over maximum accessibility, and where simultaneous users are not involved, it should be seriously considered. As reports of successful installations at the Library of Congress, the John Crerar/University of Chicago Science Library, the University of Illinois, and even this author's science library are studied, librarians may gain sufficient confidence to try them.

AISLES IN A SHELVING AREA

There is a general tension in stack layouts that involves the freedom of movement for library customers. There are the comfortable walkways of the college campus library and the packed aisles of the efficient records-management approach. The first style clearly remains appropriate in large academic special libraries — 40 percent of all the U.S. special libraries. It is also right for those large corporate headquarters or federal libraries where a substantial number of users come from some distance, many of them seeking a place to stay while consulting materials. By contrast, in those facilities where the collection is used directly by only a small group of librarians who then disburse photocopies or provide phone-in service, there can be far less seating and fewer and narrower aisles, allowing only rolling compact storage shelving.

Specification of traffic aisle width and numbers depend on the amount and frequency of two-way traffic flow. For example, in a very busy traffic aisle dividing two stack ranges, a 5-foot width might allow people to pass without literally rubbing shoulders. In academic libraries there is a tradition of at least two 3- to 4-foot traffic aisles. This reduces shelving capacity to allow easy traffic flow (see Figure 9.6A and B).

In most smaller special libraries there is less traffic. A single 3- or 4-foot traffic aisle is sufficient. Library customers can step aside into a cross aisle while another customer passes. See Figure 9.6C for an efficient shelving layout.

Cross-aisle width, the amount of space between stacks, is almost religiously specified at 36 inches, particularly in light of wheelchair access and some building codes. As a practical matter, though, almost anyone can comfortably browse in 30 inches. Allowing for one patron passing another in a cross aisle is not necessary. Again, it is so inconvenient at even 36 inches that most customers simply back out of the aisle and proceed around by another route. Or they wait patiently out in the traffic aisle as an automatic matter of social courtesy. The one good argument for the 36-inch cross aisle comes from the greater options it gives when combined with seating, consultation space, or even another bookcase, in dead-end aisles.

POSTS AND SERVICE SHAFTS IN A SHELVING AREA

Real working spaces usually pose some obstacles. Most commonly, there are posts (or columns) and service shafts. Posts cause some headaches even as they prevent others by keeping the building from collapsing down upon you. Service shafts usually bring air, heat, plumbing, electric power, or elevator service to floors above you.

In large libraries with individual floors having more than 2000 or 3000 square feet, it is not unusual to have dozens of posts in a repeating sequence. Linking any four posts on a floorplan gives the librarian rectangular spaces called modules or bays, which in large libraries circumscribe blocks of shelving or seating. A number of involved formulae are possible to optimize layouts, but, as a practi-

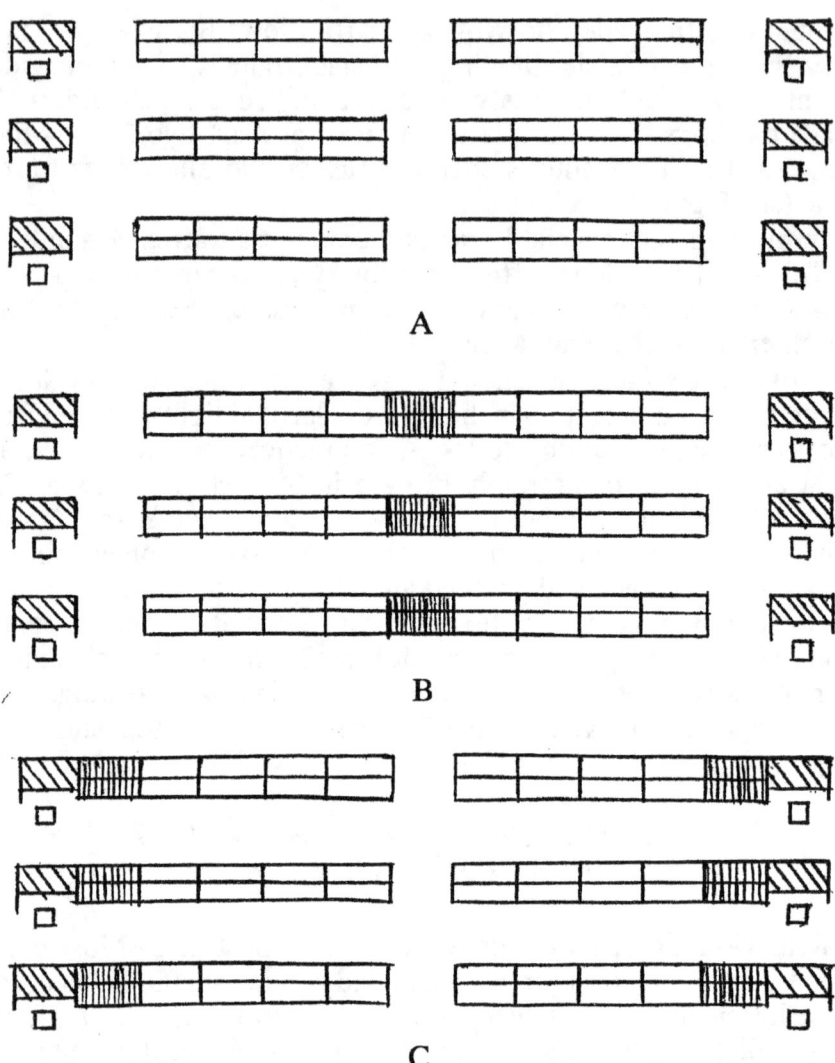

FIGURE 9.6A through C. There is a general tradeoff between ease of pedestrian traffic flow, which is enhanced by many traffic aisles, as in A, and efficiency in housing as many volumes as possible. B trades off one traffic aisle for 6 more single-face cases (see darkest shading). C trades off 2 traffic aisles for 12 more single-face cases (again, see darkest shading). Dead-end study carrels as seen in C are common in special libraries where the clientele are typically adult users doing intensive study.

cal matter, in most small special libraries adjustments for posts and shafts can be made in light of three examples.

— If the posts are small (18-inch squares or smaller), they can be allowed to intrude somewhat on the edge of a traffic aisle. A traffic aisle can be pinched from 4 feet to 3 feet every 18 feet or so without unduly constricting traffic or causing the loss of shelving units (see Figure 9.7A).
— Both stack capacity and freedom of movement are compromised by repeated intrusions of posts much larger than 18 inches into either traffic or cross aisles. These obscure access to shelves nearby and require walking around circuitously. It is generally wiser to relocate the central aisle, and rearrange the cross-aisle width somewhat so that each post is incorporated within a stack range (see Figure 9.7B).
— The handling of a service shaft in a stack area is influenced by its size. A shaft can provide good shelving if it substantially exceeds three feet in width, particularly if the shaft is square. One can wrap single-faced bookcases around it, creating an island of shelving. An additional benefit is noise softening. Books serve as excellent dampers of vibrations from ventilation and elevator shafts. It is better to put a single run of bound periodicals or other uniform material there than to use the shaft for a regular sequence of shelving. Shafts occurring in more public areas can be used for a very adequate new book display, and even for the current display of small journal collections (see Figure 9.7C).

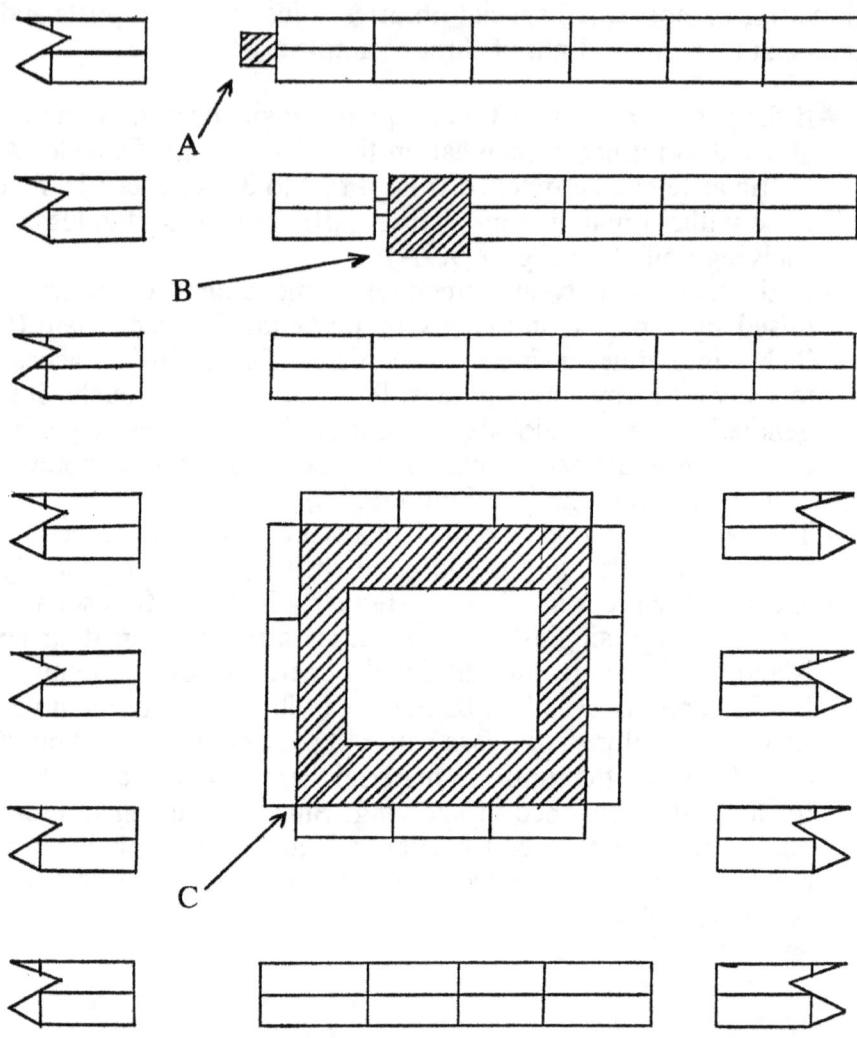

FIGURE 9.7A through C. The larger the obstruction that a post or pillar presents, the more likely a rearrangement of stack formation or aisle placement will be necessary. A represents an obstruction of a foot or less. It can be allowed to intrude on a central traffic aisle with little damage to safety or pedestrian flow. B indicates that a larger obstruction, up to about two feet, is best handled by incorporating it within a sequence of shelving, away from the busiest traffic aisle. C shows that a very large obstruction, like a utility shaft, can often be wrapped with single-faced shelving. A uniform run of materials, such as extensive holdings of a single important bound periodical, is best assigned to a shelving island such as this.

Chapter 10

The Role of the Interior Designer in Library Planning

John C. Mudgett

Creating a successful library is more than architecture, or engineering, or interior design. It is a multi-disciplinary effort that coordinates the design and problem-solving capabilities of all three disciplines to create a space for people. With a team of professionals working together, rather than in isolation, design ideas can be tested and refined, and potential problems can be avoided. The final design can be a truly integrated solution that meets the library's needs, functions smoothly and productively, and provides a pleasant work environment for its staff and users.

A primary reason for involving the interior designer at the earliest stages of planning is to draw on the designer's capabilities as a space planner. The interior designer brings a different but complementary perspective to the architectural planning process. The difference is often one of scale. While the architect generally is concerned with the whole of the building—its exterior, the relationship of its spaces and the integration of its systems—the interior designer's concerns lie with the individual user of the building, and interior spaces that function properly for that user. Effective interior design must always support the people inhabiting and the functions taking place in the designed environment.

The process of interior design parallels that of architectural design. Rather than review an essentially similar process here, we

---

Mr. Mudgett is Director of Interior Design at the architectural firm CUH2A, 600 Alexander Road, CN-5240, Princeton, NJ 08543.

plan to focus on some of the issues that must be addressed by the librarian and interior designer in the design of a new library. For a detailed review of the design process, we refer you to Chapter 6.

QUANTITATIVE ISSUES OF LIBRARY DESIGN

Space planning and interior design of libraries is an intensive process, much more so than the design of typical corporate office space. Libraries are special places with special requirements, and no two are alike. The space allocated to a library is almost always less than what is truly needed. Add to this the fact the libraries are increasingly equipment intensive and that library needs are constantly changing. The design of such a space becomes a real challenge for the interior designer and the librarian.

These are the quantitative issues of library design. They deal with the location of functional areas, the types and quantities of space, the location and accommodation of equipment, the types of lighting, and other mechanical and electrical support systems the library requires. Computerization, collection growth and lighting are currently among the most important quantitative issues.

THE GROWING IMPACT OF COMPUTERS

No single piece of equipment has had greater effect on library design than the computer. It has special lighting requirements; it has high electrical requirements; it requires additional space; it requires special furniture.

If computers are to be used by library patrons, how and where will they be used? In one of the libraries we designed recently, the decision to computerize the card catalog and to provide computer-terminal access to users for research tasks was made after initial design had been completed. This change in functional plans for the library resulted in the redesign of substantial portions of the facility.

If computers are to be used on staff members' desks, larger and lower work surfaces will be needed. Traditional desks and typewriter returns are inadequate for computer terminal use. Desktops are too high; typewriter returns are too shallow. In addition, a fully configured computer—terminal, keyboard and printer—requires substantial space. The traditional 30-inch × 60-inch work surface is inadequate to accommodate a computer and paper-and-pencil tasks.

Many libraries have computerized their card catalogs by retrofitting space previously occupied by traditional card catalogs. The inadequacies of this solution are known to virtually every librarian who has lived through the experience. Electrical, space, work surface and lighting requirements are critical considerations for computers, and they differ substantially from non-computerized environments.

ACCOMMODATING GROWING COLLECTIONS

In many rapidly growing scientific fields, current periodicals are the primary source of information. How will these collections be accommodated? Bound periodicals may be a short-term solution, but their space requirements after five years may be totally unacceptable. If microfilm is to be the primary means of storage, space requirements will be reduced, but other design considerations emerge. How many reader/printers will be needed to provide adequate access for the user population? Microfilm readers require specialized work areas. They have electrical and ventilating requirements that must be planned into the initial design of the library. They have special lighting requirements. Location near windows or uncontrolled daylight should be avoided because of glare on the screens. In addition, the noise associated with their use makes it necessary to isolate them from other areas of the library that require quiet.

To further complicate the question, are alternative forms of storage being considered for the future? For example, what will the role of online databases or the emerging technology of optical disk storage be in five years? All of these are planning considerations for the architecture and interior design team to consider at the outset.

LIGHTING: FUNCTIONAL, ESTHETIC, AND CRITICAL

The days of ceiling-mounted fluorescent lighting as the only source of light in a library are long gone. Lighting is particularly important in libraries and must be designed to accommodate specialized needs in varying areas, ranging from proper lighting of stacks to adequate lighting of computer environments.

Each functional area of the library has its own requirements. Stacks, for example, require precise alignment and spacing of ceiling fixtures to adequately illuminate shelves and aisles. If lighting is ceiling mounted and is parallel to the stacks, future changes in the arrangement of stacks will seriously compromise the quality of lighting in that area. Ceiling-mounted lighting is also expensive to change. To preserve flexibility for future space planning changes, we have successfully used lighting that is attached to the stacks, rather than mounted in the ceiling.

As computer terminals become more prevalent in library settings, other changes in lighting design are required. The ceiling-mounted fluorescent lighting that is typical of libraries and offices is totally inadequate for computer environments because of the glare it produces on VDT screens. Indirect lighting, supplemented by task lighting is usually the best solution in this environment.

These lighting issues are best resolved as part of the total planning process, not as an afterthought. As lighting systems are discussed and decisions are made with/by the planning team, the information should be coordinated with the designers of the engineering systems to ensure that the library's support systems will accommodate needs.

DESIGNING FOR CHANGE

Unlike the staid environment of the past, a library is not a static facility; it is constantly growing and changing. While all three of the previous issues argue for flexibility, we would like to caution librarians about excessive flexibility. Flexibility is required, but it must be sensibly planned. Flexibility is expensive; it should be designed into the plan only where needed.

QUALITATIVE DESIGN ISSUES

What is often more important than the quantitative issues are the qualitative issues of library design: the determination of the library's role and the development of a design that allows the library to achieve its objectives.

Libraries house research materials and equipment, but they are primarily places for people. It is the human issues that play the greatest role in determining a library's success. The library poses a special design challenge, because it must be designed for two types of people, library staff and users. Each group has its own requirements, and both need to interact yet be separated from each other. Successful accommodation of these sometimes conflicting needs is one of the interior designer's major goals.

STAFF/USER INTERACTION

In a library that serves a scientific or research facility, the librarian and staff are catalysts for the creative research process. They must be accessible to the library's users, but they also require privacy for their own administrative work and for research assignments they are undertaking. These two types of needs pose a conflict.

Each member of the library's professional staff requires a private work area, yet the work area needs to be accessible to encourage the interaction that fosters the research process. In one library we designed recently, this privacy/interaction dilemma was resolved by providing the library's research staff with a physically separate office area that was visible to library users. A floor-to-ceiling oak trellis created a physical barrier between research staff and users that still provided visibility and allowed the research staff to feel that they were a part of the activity of the rest of the library. In another special library we designed the separation was accomplished with a glass wall.

SPECIALIZED WORK SPACES

Careful attention needs to be given to the design of individual work spaces for library staff and users. Because the tasks performed and the equipment they require are more varied and complex than in the general office environment, every work area and office in the library must be designed for the specific needs of its occupant. As a result, the interior designer will probably need to work closely with each member of the library's professional staff to develop individual work areas that function properly and are comfortable, yet fit within the overall requirements of the library.

For example, in one library we recently designed, a staff member spent several hours each day engaged in research at a microfilm reader. The space allocated for the microfilm reader in the new library was very small. We worked with the researcher to custom design a microfilm research area that provided her with a comfortable working environment that met her personal needs, within the allotted space. She preferred to work seated at a Balens chair. We designed custom millwork countertops to accommodate the lower working height (about 24 inches) that this individual's requirements dictated. We also built drawers into either side of the unit for microfilm storage. The height of the work surface is adjustable, so that it can easily accommodate future users with different counter height requirements.

This is the type of thought and planning that should go into every special area of the library, from computer terminals that are used by library patrons and staff for hours of database research, to card catalog areas.

Every aspect and detail of the library should support the research process. The goals of the library can be supported or undermined by details as small as the type of furniture that is provided for users. Study carrels, for example, are best for independent, short-term research. If library users are often engaged in long-term research projects, small, private work rooms that can be reserved for extended periods may be an important feature of the library.

SIGNAGE: GOOD DIRECTIONAL SYSTEMS ENCOURAGE USE

One other area of importance to the user that is often regarded as an afterthought is signage. In a library that attempts to encourage its users to browse and find their own way to materials, an effective directional system is required. The planning and graphic look of the library's signage system should be a part of the interior design program to ensure that it enhances the overall interior design program, and it should be flexible enough to grow and change with the library.

CREATING SPECIAL PLACES

Research libraries are no longer regarded strictly as repositories of information. They have become special places. In corporations, in particular, libraries often take on a symbolic meaning as a physical manifestation of corporate commitment to research.

As a final major design consideration, libraries are often designed to achieve objectives that do not appear directly related to the library's traditional function. In several corporate libraries we have designed, the libraries became social places by design. This is a growing trend that requires sensitive planning to accommodate a non-traditional use of library space, while enhancing the library's primary function.

ENHANCING USER SPACE

Good design can create secondary roles for library space that serve corporate and library objectives. In the four most recent libraries we have designed to serve large corporate research complexes, a primary objective was to foster casual communication (and the exchange of creative ideas) among research scientists who normally work in fairly sterile and isolated laboratory environments. As a central resource for each of these research and development facilities, the library became one of the prime opportunities to achieve this objective.

As the interior designer, we translated the objective of increased casual communication into a current periodicals section in each library that featured soft, comfortable furniture grouped in conversational areas; low tables; warm, inviting finishes; and relaxing views. Our goal was to create a space that would draw people from different areas of the facility by providing a completely different environment and experience from their work areas.

The periodicals section was chosen because, of all library areas, it is the one that will permit the most activity and conversation. Users of a current periodicals section expect and require less privacy and quiet than people engaged in serious, long-term research. They tend to browse or skim materials and stay for only brief periods of time. This section of the library is also one of the few places in a large research facility where people from different departments come together. Creating a setting that subtly supports the notion of having a conversation can result in useful exchanges of information between departments that would not occur otherwise. Many times, casual exchanges have resulted in the discovery that research being conducted in one area of the company supports or validates research in another part.

THE DESIGN PROCESS

We have raised some of the more important current issues in library design and have shown by example how they were accommodated with several specific examples. This is the interior designer's greatest value, but the designer provides other services to the librarian after the plans have been developed.

One of the functions of the interior designer is to utilize modern methods of making working drawings understandable to the client. For example, data entered into a computer-assisted design and drafting (CADD) system can be manipulated to provide a variety of three-dimensional views of the library. A two-dimensional floor plan (Figure 10.1) comes to life in a three-dimensional CADD drawing (Figure 10.2) that shows a view of the library from the exterior wall behind the chairs.

Raising issues and resolving them is the heart of the programming and design process. As issues are resolved, the design be-

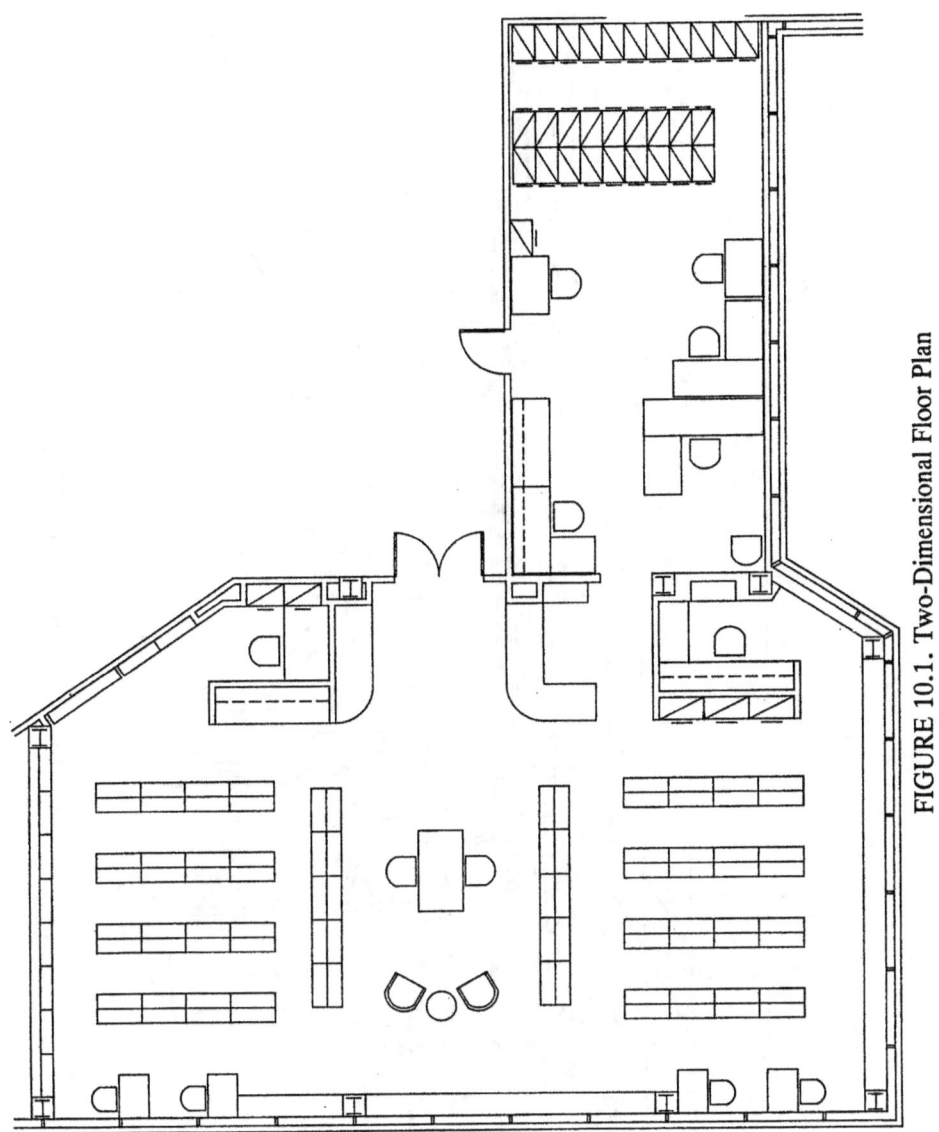

FIGURE 10.1. Two-Dimensional Floor Plan

FIGURE 10.2. Three-Dimensional Floor Plan

comes clearer and clearer. By the end of the design process, the designer will be able to present to the librarian a detailed space plan, office and workstation diagrams, furniture plans, special area designs, and all interior finishes and materials. Once these are approved, the designer prepares a detailed written specification of all furnishings, as well as working drawings and other documentation needed to fully describe the interior design portion of the library project in order to obtain competitive bidding on labor and material. These specifications are normally provided to the client for direct purchase. The designer usually assists the client in selecting bidders and in negotiating with dealers, but does not act as purchasing agent.

The interior designer remains active during the construction and installation phases of the library. Field visits are made at regular intervals to inspect the construction of the interior. The designer also assists the library's staff in planning and coordinating the move to the new facilities.

On completion of construction, the interior designer assists the librarian in preparing a preliminary punch list, which lists deficiencies in installation or construction that must be repaired or completed by the contractor or vendor. After move-in, the interior designer monitors the progress of the preliminary punch list, and formulates a final punch list. Most interior designers also make their services available after the library has moved into its new facilities, to remedy any post-occupancy problems that occur.

FINISHING TOUCHES

Yes, color, fabric and furniture selections still are the province of the interior designer, but they are only a small part of what the interior designer does. Selection of colors, finishes, and style are a part of the process, and have aesthetic importance. They help the library to achieve its objectives as a place for people. But the most significant skills brought to library planning by the interior designer will be the planning skills that ensure that the library will meet the needs of its staff, its users, and the corporation or institution that it serves when it is built and through the years as it grows and changes.

Chapter 11

Furnishing the Electronic Library

Lorraine Schulte

For most of us without architectural training or three-dimensional imaging abilities, the step from the two-dimensional blueprint to the reality of the completed library facility is a huge one. What is it really going to look like? The less experience we have with making the transition from blueprint squares and rectangles to chairs, tables, and other furnishings that we can see and feel, the more uneasy we are about making the decisions that will make this happen. Although the blueprint is the critical foundation, some very important decisions about furnishing contribute significantly to the overall success of the library. Here the art of library planning takes over from the science of space-need projections, blueprint specifications, and engineering drawings.

A little bit of creativity in furnishing the library can turn a rather straightforward library design into a warm and welcoming or stimulating facility. The same blueprint layout can produce entirely different results depending on the interior design plan developed for the facility. The look and feel a planner wants to create in furnishing the library information center will depend upon its organizational philosophy and goals, the business of the parent organization, and the corporate culture in general.

Creative problem-solving through furnishing is a must when dealing with structural limitations unavoidable in the original planning, for example, mechanical space in undesirable places, not enough outside light or too much of it, the need to balance a feeling

---

Ms. Schulte is Director, Corporate Technical Library, Upjohn Company, 7171 Portage Road, Kalamazoo, MI 49001.

of openness and accessibility with the need for privacy and noise control.

The gradual increase in the variety and quantity of electronic products in the typical special library brings with it the need for those involved in planning modern libraries to consider several problems that didn't exist before computers and similar equipment became commonplace. The very fact that the problems are relatively new forces the planner to think creatively about such matters, since not a great deal of past experience has been accumulated and since the need for good-looking, functional, and lasting solutions is important.

The stage for selecting furnishings usually occurs sometime well after construction starts. By this time a vision of the completed library information center and of the changes that might impact the facility five to ten years after occupancy is already developed. Although some changes are possible to anticipate, a fair amount of unpredictability still exists. Given these conditions, flexibility is central to furnishing the library information center interior. Although maximum flexibility is most desirable in an environment of constant change, some compromises in reaching this goal will avoid inflated cost and perhaps even loss in esthetic value.

This chapter reviews some of the basics related to creating the general library environment, such as heating, ventilating, air conditioning, ceilings, walls, floors, wiring, and lighting. It then discusses furnishing in sections on furniture and equipment for user space, service areas, office areas, and special areas to support computers, electronic workstations, and online training.

THE BASICS

The General Environment

The mission of the library information center, its current resources, and its long-range plans dictate the amount of space necessary for a new library facility. Physical building limitations, monetary constraints, and other realities operating in the plan of the parent organization often temper these planning projections. A special library infrequently occupies a building of its own, except perhaps in the case of very large academic special libraries, e.g., biomedical or science libraries. The larger building project of which a special library is a part therefore determines many of its environmental features.

The person responsible for the final phases of furnishing the library interior has more influence over other environmental basics such as smoking, noise control, etc. Non-smoking facilities are more and more common by choice and by law, providing a healthy environment and eliminating many problems of electronic equipment and physical plant maintenance.

Early in the design phase, some form of sound-masking white noise warrants consideration, especially if open-plan offices are to be part of the library information center. White noise can help mask the noise of voices and hubbub in core service areas from the more quieter study areas.

Many basic environmental features and considerations are the same in an electronic or highly automated library as in the traditional, more paper-oriented, library. Parts of the environment that need special consideration because of the arrival of the electronic office and the electronic library are heat, humidity, wiring, and lighting.

Heating, Ventilating, and Air Conditioning

Electronic workstations, audiovisual equipment, and computers, in addition to whatever they contribute to library operations and services, contribute significantly to the heat-load in the environment. Although the newer generation computing equipment and electronic workstations are manufactured so that they generate less heat, the thermal output of this equipment is still a factor, along with lighting and other electronic equipment, as a source of heat for the entire building. Knowledge of the specific heat-generating capacity of electronic equipment being installed in a library facility or office area is important, especially when considering closed spaces where another factor is limited ventilation. Open-landscape office designs ameliorate some of these concerns as the heat from the electronic workstations diffuses over a larger area. Heating, ventilation, and air conditioning (HVAC) facilities in small modular units allow maximum flexibility in office arrangements and rearrangements. The modular approach avoids problems of office walls and partitions sealing off or segregating access to HVAC facilities.

In new building construction, proper humidity controls should minimize any problems with inadequate or excessive moisture. Certain types of photocopy equipment will not function well without sufficient humidity (not always the same as the humidity preferred by the human occupants of the facility). Static electricity from inadequate moisture can interfere with the proper functioning of electronic equipment. Discharged through a person onto a video display terminal, static electricity can alter or erase the display or even alter the programming instructions on the computer chips, depending on how effective the grounding is for electrical equipment. In older buildings being remodeled, inadequate humidity may indicate the need for special carpet manufactured to provide some form of static electricity control. Application of special carpet sprays after installation will also reduce static electricity if humidity control is not possible.

Ceilings, Walls, and Floors

The library information center environment contains many sub-environments, all of which may allow different treatments to the ceiling area. An unfinished ceiling in the stack area, where the conduit, ducts, and pipes remain uncovered, can provide significant economies. In one approach to the ceiling, black paint makes all of the utility services plus the wall and ceiling immediately above them disappear. The lighting suspended below these services then creates an apparent ceiling. In another approach, bright paint highlights the utility services to break up the overly regimented environment of the stacks. Ceiling tiles in open-plan office areas must have appropriate sound absorption capabilities to reduce ambient noise in this type of environment.

Whether walls are masonry, block, dry wall, or glass will influence not only the placement of offices and library furnishings, but may also require consideration of materials to either mask or enhance sound or light created by these materials. The choice in flooring is more and more often a low-pile carpet, especially in smaller library information centers. Low-pile, glued carpet, and large-caster book trucks seem to eliminate concerns about rolling book trucks on carpet. Carpet, a key contributor to sound absorption, increases flexibility when it covers the entire floor, even under the stacks. Carpet cut out and laid around stacks makes the stacks permanent features unless the plan calls for the expense of future recarpeting. The choice of carpet, whether carpet squares or broadloom, has proponents on both sides. Carpet squares, glued down but still easily moved because of their adhesive qualities, allow flat wire to be laid beneath them. Pulling them up makes possible a rearrangement of wiring and equipment and merely tacking the carpet squares down again covers the relocated wire. Not all wiring in an electronic library, however, will lend itself to flat wire form; the coaxial cable for computer connections is still not flat. Although carpet squares allow for easy replacement of badly damaged or worn carpet, newer squares with unworn pile may still stand out in contrast to previously laid carpet. Remember that carpeting on walls and other structures serves for both appearance and sound absorption. Previous comments about the color and patterns for carpeting in regard to showing soil should be kept in mind.

Wiring

The larger construction project for the building housing the library information center may dictate whether conduit for wiring goes into ducts under the floor, at the perimeter, or within the ceiling. Wiring location may, therefore, be out of the library's control. Under-floor ducts eliminate the need for unsightly power poles and the same duct will handle electrical conduit, coaxial cables, cables for local area networks (LANS), twisted-pair wiring for telephone, and fiber optic cables. The potential for wiring outlets just about everywhere would be ideal but quite expensive. The closer we get to this goal, however, the better able the library information center will be to provide for electrical and communications facilities anywhere within its space, now and in the future. Every office and every library service station should be equipped with the capability for supporting electronic workstations and communications.

Construction of any new office building in the eighties occurs with a heightened awareness of the electronic nature of the typical office environment. Corporations and universities are installing their own telephone systems or local area networks, e.g., Ethernet, for internal computer communications. The construction engineer, however, may still underestimate the electrical hubbub the typical library represents. It is truly a communications center. Therefore, early on, the library planner should prepare a list of all equipment by type, quantity, location, and required number of outlets. Next comes planning for special circuits, power supplies required by specific equipment, and requirements for special dedicated lines, e.g., OCLC or leased communications connections to book and journal vendors. An uninterrupted power supply and surge controls are also important for sensitive computer workstations.

Audiovisual or media viewing areas planned for the library information center, or rooms for user education and training on electronic information systems (see the section on Online Training Center), will generate special electrical needs. Further discussion of electrical and communications requirements for the typical library office and user areas will follows in other sections of this chapter.

Lighting

The structure of the building and its window locations largely determine natural lighting in a library. These may be beyond the range of the library planner's influence. Whether a great deal of natural light is available, whether tinted windows modify the heating as well as the lighting effects of natural light, whether skylights and atriums are present, or whether any outside light is available are all factors that influence interior design, stack locations, and selection of furnishings for the library information center.

There are functional as well as a esthetic reasons to have varied lighting in different areas of the library. Over the years lighting requirements for typical library reading and stack areas have been the topic of much literature (see the Bibliography at the end of this chapter). Today we have new concerns for special lighting requirements dictated by the almost ubiquitous video display terminals (VDT). Lighting that allows glare-free reading of information on VDT screens should be available in all areas with study carrels, offices, and library service stations, e.g., the reference desk, circulation desk, online catalog stations. Fluorescent lighting with parabolic or Fresnel lenses markedly reduces the glare problem.

Immediately over library stack areas, more traditional forms of lighting might be satisfactory. In major public areas like the entry and core-service areas, consider special lighting for distinguishing these areas with some dramatic effect. The latter, however, should never override the concern for functionality. The lighting has to work.

Furniture

Furniture and furnishings are a significant part of the total interior design, plan which is the primary subject of Chapter 10. The interior design, budget, institutional prerequisites, and institutional vendor preferences all have a part to play in choosing furniture.

As the electronic workstation, computers, and computer peripherals proliferated throughout the office world, office furniture manufacturers and other special equipment manufacturers responded with more and more furniture designed to meet the special electrical and other logistical requirements of offices with this electronic equipment. Nevertheless, there is still a place for the library furniture manufacturer. Because the library furniture business serves such a specialized market and smaller runs are the basis for cost, it is not unusual to obtain customized modifications at relatively little additional cost. The same modifications to items in the standard catalogs of large office furniture manufacturers could be extremely costly or out of the question. Library furniture manufacturers are better able to provide the functionality required in special purpose furniture, such as circulation desks, reference desks, study carrels, etc. Even if the library furniture manufacturer does not accommodate all of the electronic needs of the modern library information center in its standard catalog of furnishings, it has the flexibility to adapt. Solving library furnishing problems, not just selling a commodity, interests the library furniture manufacturer. The library design skills of the manufacturer's representative can contribute a great deal to resolve problems with the facility and fill special furnishing needs. Specially designed pieces might be required, created in toto for the library customer, or major and minor modifications to existing pieces of furniture. The vision of the library professional is still vital, however, to ensure that library furnishings meet interior design requirements and the challenges of the electronic library into the next ten or more years.

Good advice to those selecting library furnishings should be available from the manufacturer, its sales representatives, and other professional colleagues. Even if the parent institution has a complex and confining bid process for obtaining furnishings, this choice should not be left to chance, to the corporate office systems planner, the best price, or the pictures in the manufacturer's catalog. It is best to go see, feel, and try out the library furniture firsthand before making a final decision. Ideally, that decision should be the library director's.

FURNITURE IN THE PUBLIC USER SPACE

Regardless of how electronic the library information center is becoming, as long as it is a resource to visit and work in, it will be a facility that supports consultation with printed library materials and a variety of study spaces, as well as utilization of electronic media and equipment. The variety of activities in themselves necessarily dictates a variety of environments and furnishings.

The idea of providing a choice of seating options appropriate for some specific function should enliven the seat selection process. Individual study carrels, small and large study tables, stools for consultation tables, and lounge chairs should all find a place somewhere in the facility. A large, open area serving as the only break in an extended range of journal stacks, suggested to one library planner a good location for a long S-shaped arrangement of sectional lounge furniture. It did look rather nice on the blueprint. Just two or three bound journals, however, lower the library customer's center of gravity into this soft lounge furniture and create seating most difficult to arise from. Other drawbacks are that it does not provide a convenient working area and writing surface. Therefore, a more formal arrangement of study tables and chairs replaced the S-shaped arrangement of lounge furniture in the plans. Lounge furniture is certainly appropriate, however, in a current journal reading area for the browsing activity that goes on there. It would also be fair today to anticipate the library customer with a portable, lap-top computer who might well enjoy sinking into a lounge chair to work with the computer as long as there were not too many other materials to work with, which would then require a larger study table surface.

Individual study carrels at a minimum 3-foot width can accommodate a small personal computer and still leave writing space available. Four-foot wide carrels might be preferable, however, assuming more of this multimedia approach to information gathering, generation, and processing will continue. At least some library information center customers are finding that working on-site with their personal computers, taking advantage of their word processing functions and access to personal and corporate databases, makes it more convenient to review bound periodical literature. They can make electronic notes immediately and not have to wait in the office or laboratory for a photocopy to arrive via the document delivery service.

The availability of small- to medium-size conference rooms with tables and chairs are important for library information center customers and staff alike. With increasing emphasis on participative management and group problem-solving, small groups of staff may frequently need discussion space. The typical conference room in the electronic library needs to be equipped far beyond tables and chairs. Telephones, overhead projectors, videotape playback equipment, computer terminals or personal computers, modems, or data communications modules (DCM) for access to internal corporate and external information resources, and perhaps even video conferencing equipment are more and more common requirements for conference room operations. Electronic photoboards are useful additions to these conference facilities in lieu of an easel and pad of newsprint. The photoboard permits immediate production of 8-1/2 × 11-inch photocopies of any material penned on its surface, thereby allowing meeting participants to walk away with their own paper copies of the board material shared in the group.

Appropriate placement of index tables, consulting tables, reference counters, and online catalog counter surfaces is also important. Consulting tables for standing or stools for sitting are appropriate in areas where library information center customers spend limited time, such as in the monographic reference collection area, at the online catalog, or in the printed index area. Fifteen years into the era of online literature searching finds regular consultation of printed indexes less and less common. Some printed versions of online indexes are no longer even added to collections. Those that are still purchased might be adequately handled in regular stacks with occasional consulting shelves. The expense of purchasing index tables and the floor-space requirements of providing indexing and abstracting tools on consulting tables are only justified in the case of a few primary indexing and abstracting tools that serve the key subject areas in the library information center collection.

While durability is a concern for all library furnishings, further evaluation of tables and work surfaces is desirable for the lasting qualities of wood versus the more common plastic laminate and for the reflective tendencies of finish and color choices. Plastic laminate is available today with color all through the material, not just on the surface, where it is subject to unsightly wear. Very light colored surfaces can create too much glare for readers, depending on the electric lighting or natural lighting in the reading area.

From tables to stools to book trucks, much traditional library furnishing is used for the electronic library. What is different is the need to select or modify this furniture so that it is capable of supporting electronic adaptations. The circulation desk, the reference desk, the online catalog stations, and study carrels all must be able to handle electronic equipment and wiring in a convenient and an esthetic manner. A simple device such as a raceway—an open space of about an inch wide running the length of the rear of work surfaces—will allow for convenient and flexible wire drops of any number and arrangement. A small vertical edge at the front of the open raceway will prevent material falling off the back of the work surface. The raceway immediately converts a typical study carrel into an electronic workstation, whether or not it comes initially equipped with wiring and outlets. The reference desk in the electronic library may have to be fairly large to accommodate the different types of equipment required for accessing a variety of electronic systems and information resources. To facilitate the placement and frequent change of terminals, printers, and personal computers at the reference desk, the open raceway is ideal.

FURNISHING EQUIPMENT SPACE

The electronic library information center is integrating information formats of many types and providing decentralized access. The evolution from the card catalog to the online catalog decentralized the catalog and caused libraries to distribute online catalog stations beyond the core area of the library information center, allowing remote access even within the same facility. The planner must select or design furniture to support these decentralized catalog stations.

As videodiscs or CD-ROM join microfilm as a storage medium for information formerly found only in printed publications and as more information appears in various audiovisual (AV) formats, it becomes even more unreasonable to expect the on-site user of these resources to travel from place to place because of format variation. Consideration of the trade-offs should precede the decision either to segregate all audiovisual or non-print materials in a separate room or to distribute them throughout the library. A separate AV room is certainly easier to prepare for ideal accommodation of audiovisual equipment: microfilm readers and reader/printers, videocassette playback equipment, slide/tape machines, CD-ROM players, etc. If these media are not big items in the library information center, a few special purpose audiovisual carrels (wet carrels with outlets) grouped in one area of the facility, somewhere near staff assistance, is another reasonable alternative. A pinwheel carrel unit is a very compact way to put four audiovisual stations in limited space.

The customer, however, would appreciate the convenience of finding all materials on a particular subject or the parts of a particular periodical title in one location, regardless of format. If the stacks hold microfilm copies of periodicals along with the printed versions, they should also contain the microfilm reader/printers. Carrel-size microfilm equipment is available, some with their own stands. A larger carrel, more typical of those supporting audiovisual equipment, might be preferable for placement of distributed microfilm reader/printers. Another consideration for microfilm reader/printer workstations—none of which seem perfectly ideal because of reading angle problems especially for the bifocal or trifocal wearer—is a work surface that will accommodate the left-handed writer as well as the right-handed person. A simple pull-out work surface on the left side of microfilm and other audiovisual carrels can make life much easier for the left-handed person.

Convenient distribution of document photocopy stations should also be a basic requirement for the library information center space. Manufacturer's requirements for minimum space to the front, back, and sides of the machine for proper functioning and maintenance may limit the placement of photocopy machines. Placement should also support the proper workflow for activity at the photocopy station. There should be a nearby storage cabinet for photocopy paper and basic supplies for cleaning and maintaining the machine, as well as a work surface for collating and stapling if the machine does not already provide this. People also need a place to leave books and periodicals after they finish copying them.

There is need to establish the relationship of other special equipment to library functions and services. Such things as Telex, telecopier equipment, search stations for special purpose computer graphics, microfilm cleaning equipment, barcode readers, and optical digital disk reader/printers must all have appropriate placement and support to fit well into the workflow. Wiring flexibility built into the entire facility makes this job much easier.

On our way from the library environment with just one 300-baud dumb terminal for online searching, to the completely electronic library accessible from remote workstations in every office and laboratory, there are several possible transitional scenarios for electronic workstation equipment integration. This provides a further challenge for alternative equipment environments within the library information center.

Already mentioned was the need to support the library information center customer who comes to the facility equipped with a personal lap-top computer to do his or her own searching or word processing. There are others who will rely totally on an information intermediary and work with this library information specialist in a team approach to online database searching. Therefore, the planner must design individual search staff offices and/or the reference desk to accommodate team searching. Still others may depend on the library information center for access to computing equipment and come there to use it. The end-user searcher may want to be near the search expertise of the library information specialist who can point to appropriate databases and guide the customer in the various techniques necessary for optimizing retrieval.

The latter kind of customer might well be served by a search laboratory within the library information center facility, a place offering a variety of computing equipment for customers: a personal computer with communications software and hardware for accessing external databases, a terminal hardwired to the mainframe computing resource, a special graphics search station for computer-assisted chemistry searches on both internal and external databases, etc. The search laboratory would ideally be located in the vicinity of the reference or information desk and/or the information specialists' offices so that assistance is readily available. The search laboratory is a place where the customer can interact with several information resources and services at one centralized location.

LIBRARY AUTOMATION

In larger organizations, more widely shared mainframe database management systems that can be adapted for library automation, or library automation systems built for mainframes already owned by the corporation, may mean off-site location of the computer supporting library automation. In this case there is no need for a special computer room immediately within the library information center facility.

As the power and storage capability of the typical mainframe becomes more and more completely approximated in the personal computer and personal computer networks, the tendency will be to support library automation software on-site. In smaller libraries, just one of the more powerful personal computers may be sufficient. But even as computing power becomes more compact, a myriad of peripheral computer support equipment may still take up a good deal of floor space. There may be value in grouping, especially the shared equipment, in a special computing facility.

Library information specialists with electronic search stations in their own offices may share a printer with others for reasons of cost saving or quality, e.g., a shared letter-quality printer supplementing an in-office draft printer. A special leased line to a heavily used database vendor permits immediate on-site printing of search results at high speeds (300 lines per minute), thereby eliminating the wait for off-site generation of larger printouts that must be mailed. Controlling the noise generated by these printers might best be accomplished by putting them into a computer room or an otherwise closed-off area. A library information center computer room might also house one of the distributed corporate mainframe printers that serves library customers and library information center staff who use off-site mainframe resources. Accommodating the location of automated system back up equipment is another need that might be served by a computing room.

Although new microprocessing technology makes the computer room less and less necessary, if the library information center requires one, there is usually much corporate or institutional experience with the requirements for such a facility. These requirements include proper cooling and humidity control for optimal functioning of the central processor and printers, warning or alarm systems for hazardous changes in temperature from failure of the cooling system, and a halon fire extinguishing system, if the cost of the computing equipment warrants it. A special computer room should provide not only heat, humidity, and dust control but typically a raised floor for the abundance of wiring that goes with all of this equipment. Furnishing the computer room also means providing storage cabinets for tapes, disks, and paper supplies.

ONLINE USER EDUCATION AND TRAINING FACILITY

Over the years library user education in special libraries evolved from the simple walking tour to classroom-based instruction in major indexing and abstracting tools, and then to online literature search or end-user training. As more formal instruction in the use of bibliographic tools, personal information management, and information resources of various types evolved, the conference room/classroom became an essential accessory to the library information center facility. Today a room equipped appropriately to handle end-user training in the use of electronic information systems may be essential to many library information centers. A classroom equipped for electronic training with all the appropriate accessory teaching tools, such as audiovisual equipment and a video projector for large screen projection of VDT images, can be a costly undertaking. In a large institution or corporation, however, there is widespread need for electronic workstation training of all sorts: for word processing; for mainframe statistical programs, database management systems, and electronic mail; for personal computers and accessory software, e.g., spread-sheet programs. An investment in a facility of this type can benefit all of these groups, and its location in the library information center area enhances the identification of the library information center as a center for information resources, information services, information management, and access to electronic information systems.

An online training facility might need to handle a variety of workstation hardware if the following are in use throughout the institution: mainframe terminals, dedicated word-processing equipment, graphics-search stations, personal computers. As the personal computer becomes increasingly widespread, so too does the availability of special purpose office furniture and electronic workstation furniture. Manufacturers provide a wide variety of individual workstation options, but locally designed and constructed millwork may also be a fairly cost-effective approach to furnishing an electronic training center. For example, a continuous work surface for multiple electronic workstations can integrate the set-up of the workstations and writing space in a functional and esthetic manner, provide superior wire handling, offer great flexibility for changes in set-up, and accommodate more students as well (four to ten per row). Beneath the work surface of such a continuous workstation design, continuous channels in the skirt or back panel can handle and hide the wiring. The ergonomic requirements of the individual in regard to the workstation are as important to consider in the classroom as in the individual office spaces (see the following section on Furnishing the Office). Ergonomically designed chairs will provide the chair height flexibility required for different size students working at an average fixed height workstation counter (usually somewhere between 29-inch desk height and 26-inch typing height).

Lighting, of course, is critical in an electronic training facility. Multiple VDT workstations must be kept free of glare. Variable light controls for various portions of the room are important to permit clear viewing of projected slides, videotapes, and video projection of VDT screen displays, while still allowing note taking.

FURNISHING THE OFFICE

The most functional office buildings today allow for frequent changes in office layout and design. This flexibility is a key element in keeping up with the frequent changes dictated by developing information technologies. Open-landscape plans, with knockdown, modular, office system partitions and workstations, find favor in many environments, both for their flexibility and for the favorable tax implications. Because this is an investment in office equipment, modular landscaped offices can depreciate faster than facilities or walls. The original investment in open-landscape partitions may in fact exceed the cost of drywall, but partitions permit frequent minor adjustments or even major rearrangements without the extended disruption and messiness involved in moving fixed walls. Open-landscape office panels usually provide excellent wire handling through a channel at the base of the panel with frequent punchouts for wire terminations; however, there are other tradeoffs. While they definitely offer visual privacy, they sacrifice acoustic privacy. Even with special sound-absorbent material on the panel faces, a large or small open-landscape area still functions best in a planned environment with masking white noise and ceiling tiles with the highest possible noise reduction coefficient (NRC value). A significant initial cost in an adequate white noise system, or other approaches to quieting conversation and machine noise, must be traded off against the continuing loss in staff productivity associated with the inability to block out distracting noise from people and equipment in nearby offices.

In the library office, as well as the public areas, it is preferable to err on the side of flexibility. We are already aware of how electronic information systems and automation support for traditional library functions are changing the way the library information center does business. This is gradually affecting the nature of jobs, merging tasks, and blurring the lines between traditional departments. Changing workflows mean positions will change, and ultimately departmental lines will change — all requiring office changes.

In many office environments, the open-landscape plan for offices involves frequent repetitions of a very few modular designs, but in the library information center this may not be appropriate. Tasks, workflow, and equipment can vary considerably from department to department and from position to position. It may well be worth the time to consider individual office plans for each job category, department, or even each position. This, of course, needs to be balanced against a tendency to create a unique person-specific office with design requirements too personalized to serve others who may fill the position. Although it is possible to redefine open-plan offices and change or rearrange modular work surfaces, this is not necessarily something to embark upon every time there is a personnel change.

The makers of modern office furniture that integrates with landscape panels have become aware of the need for ergonomically designed furnishings to support work in the electronic office. Secretary, clerk, professional, manager — all spend considerable time at an electronic workstation of some sort. Desk chairs must appropriately support long hours in front of a screen and keyboard, as well as reading and writing positions. Placement of detachable work surfaces in one of these modular offices can be at desk height (29-inches) or at the lower typing height (26-inches). To avoid too many post-occupancy changes, it is very useful to develop a mock-up of some of the open-plan office modules and to list equipment required in each office.

Although the typical new office today may have what seems to be an abundance of electrical outlets, their location must match the need to use them. It may be surprising, for instance, to count what the typical secretarial office might include in the way of plug-in equipment: task lights (one or more), typewriter, word processor, printer, dictation transcriber, pencil sharpener, clock, calculator, dataphone power unit, electric stapler. The secretarial office with eight duplex outlets (16 receptacles) may seem more than adequately equipped. If two duplex outlets are distributed to each wall, however, they will not support the majority of secretarial equipment located against the one wall constituting the secretary's primary workplace. Because integration of computer systems is not yet complete, and one universal electronic workstation to support all systems does not yet exist, terminals, modems, printers, PCs, and multiple versions of these combine to add greater challenge to the task of providing adequate electric outlets for the typical library office.

OTHER CONSIDERATIONS

There are a number of little things that are easy to forget in furnishing the library information center. Without appropriate attention to their total integration with the overall interior design, they can detract from the final appearance of the facility.

In the modern library information center, storage means not only adequate out-of-the way space for extra bookends, Princeton files, jiffy bags, and paper supplies of various types but also hardware and software manuals, manufacturer's operating instructions, backup hardware, and even hardware or equipment for circulation. There has probably never been a facility with too much storage space for these kinds of things.

Waste cans, pencil sharpeners, step stools, bulletin boards, display units, and racks for handouts should be compatible with the overall style and color scheme selected for the interior design. The color scheme also should apply to the selection of even desk top office furnishings like staplers and in-boxes. Decorative art, as the final touch, can mean a lot in the attempt to balance a very high-tech environment, having a potentially hard feeling, with the softer lines of fabric, sculpture, painting, and other art objects. Supporting local artists may put the purchase of original art well within the budget for the new facility.

All of this advance design and furnishing effort means the final product usually pleases library planners who would like to maintain its original appearance as long as possible. Proper maintenance and strict adherence to original design, style, and color schemes can make this possible. Upholstery, as well as carpeting, needs regular cleaning. Designation of certain staff for regular troubleshooting, inspecting, and discovering the need for special repairs should increase an overall awareness of the appearance of the facility. Most important to the long-term security and integrity of the facility is a disaster plan that provides for quick response to mitigate various dangers such as fire, smoke, and water.

The one thing we face with certainty in the future of the information society is more change: change within the library information center, its resources and services; change within and between library departments caused by integrated automation systems; change brought about by the maturing of institutional or corporate information resource management. Changes in information resource management may bring about new relationships and even further merging of information departments now quite separate from each other. The library information center planned with maximum flexibility and electronic capacity should be very capable of meeting these challenges.

REFERENCES

Beckman, Margaret. Library buildings in the network environment. *Journal of Academic Librarianship*. 9(5):281-284; 1983.

Blackburn, Robert H. Automation and building plans. In: *Reader on the library building*. Schell, Hal B., ed. Englewood, CO: Microcard Editions Books; 1975:266-272.

Blackwell, H. Richard. Lighting the library—standards for illumination. In: *Reader on the library building*. Schell, Hal B., ed. Englewood, CO: Microcard Editions Books; 1975:213-222.

Chan, David F.C. Computerizing the small library: equipment and other considerations. In: *The library in the information revolution: Proceedings of the sixth congress of Southeast Asian Libraries*; 1983. Singapore: Maruzen Asia Pte Ltd.; 1983: Chapter 12: 121-127.

Cohen, Elaine; Cohen, Aaron. *Automation, space management & productivity: a guide for librarians*. New York: R.R. Bowker Co.; 1981.

Cohen, Elaine; Cohen, Aaron. *Library automation & facility planning*. ERIC; 1980: 280p. ED 256346.

Cohen, Elaine; Cohen, Aaron. *Library planning*. New York: Aaron Cohen Associates; 1980.

Crouch, C.L. More light on lighting—too much light is poor light. In: *Reader on the library building*. Schell, Hal B., ed. Englewood, CO: Microcard Editions Books; 1975. 233-234.

de Bear, Richard. Planning the electronic library. In: *Managing the electronic library: Papers of the 1982 conference of the Library Management Division of Special Libraries Association*; 1982. Koenig, Michael, ed. New York: Special Libraries Association; 1983: 26-31.

Epstein, Susan Baerg. Implementation—preparing the site. *Library Journal*. 108(20):2142-2143; 1983 November.

Fraley, Ruth A; Anderson, Carol Lee. *Library space planning: How to assess, allocate, and reorganize collections, resources, and physical facilities*. New York: Neal-Schuman Publishers; 1985.

Grad, Ian; Greenberg, Alfred. Air conditioning for books and people. In: *Reader on the library building*. Schell, Hal B., ed. Englewood, CO: Microcard Editions Books; 1975: 242-248.

Heathcote, Denis; Stubley, Peter. Building services and environmental needs of information technology in academic libraries. Program: Automated Library and Information Systems. 20(1):26-38; 1986 January.

Hodge, M. Patricia; Lawrence, Barbara. Planning for the electronic library. In: *Managing the electronic library: Papers of the 1982 conference of the Library Management Division of Special Libraries Association*. Koenig, Michael, ed. New York: Special Libraries Association; 1983. 13-25.

Holland, Gloria J. [and others]. A checklist for planning and designing audiovisual facilities in health sciences libraries. *Bulletin of the Medical Library Association*. 72(4):362-369; 1984 October.

Information technology and space planning. *Library Systems Newsletter*. 5(11): 81-83; 1985.

Jordan, Robert T. More light on lighting—cost is an irrelevant factor. In: *Reader on the library building*. Schell, Hal B., ed. Englewood, CO: Microcard Editions Books; 1975: 228-230.

Lam, William M.C. More light on lighting—observe light, evaluate reports. *In: Reader on the library building*. Schell, Hal B., ed. Englewood, CO: Microcard Editions Books; 1975: 231-232.

Mason, Ellsworth. A guide to the librarian's responsibility in achieving quality in lighting and ventilation. In: *Reader on the library building*. Schell, Hal B., ed. Englewood, CO: Microcard Editions Books; 1975: 235-241.

Matthews, Joseph R. Installing the computer. In: *Choosing an automated library system: a planning guide*. Chicago: American Library Association; 1980: Chapter 6.

Metcalf, Keyes D. Library lighting. In: *Reader on the library building*. Schell, Hal B., ed. Englewood, CO: Microcard Editions Books; 1975: 223-227.

Moriarty, John H. New media facilities. In: *Reader on the library building*. Schell, Hal B., ed. Englewood, CO: Microcard Editions Books; 1975: 249-253.

Parkhurst, C.A. Choosing an automated library; site requirements and system maintenance. Chicago: American Library Association; 1983: 64-70.

Pierce, William S. *Furnishing the library interior*. New York: Marcel Dekker; 1980.
Pinder, Chris; Storey, Colin. Green light for new technology? The ergonomics of automation. *Library Association Record*. 88(6):282-283, 285; 1986.
Rohlf, Robert H. Building-planning implications of automation. In: *Reader on the library building*. Schell, Hal B., ed. Englewood, CO: Microcard Editions Books; 1975: 261-265.
Roose, Tina. Ergonomics in the library. *Library Journal*. 111(17):54-55; 1986.
Schell, Hal B., ed. *Reader on the library building*. Englewood, CO: Microcard Editions Books; 1975.
Segesta, James. Pulling the rug out from under the stacks. *College & Research Libraries News*. 47(7): 441-444; 1986.

Chapter 12

An Annotated Bibliography on Planning Special Libraries

Beverly S. Gordon

The following annotated bibliography represents a selective list of references chosen for their usefulness in the planning of special libraries and information centers.

In the period since the boom in library building of the 1960s and early 1970s, there has been an increased emphasis on more efficient space and resource utilization. The major impact on changing the appearance of libraries has been the technological advances reflected in automation, microcomputers, new types of media, and new information technologies. Conventional library furniture and equipment has remained unchanged and the number of manufacturers has dramatically decreased, while new kinds of furniture and equipment have become prominent in libraries and a new group of vendors has developed. A brief review of library events for the past year, including such topics as buildings, furniture and equipment, and security can be found in the *ALA Yearbook of Library and Information Services*.

These changes in library planning are reflected in the current library literature. While an attempt has been made to include the most recent material available, this was easier for some topics than for others. Generally, materials for inclusion were taken from the period within the last ten years. Thus, this bibliography serves to

---

Beverly S. Gordon is a free-lance librarian, living at 62-30 Clyde Street, Apt. 5 E, Forest Hills, NY 11375.
  Appreciation is due for the assistance given by Teresa Wyman in locating certain literature for consideration in this bibliography.

update the one by Janice A. Kreider covering through 1970 and published in *Planning the Special Library* (SLA Monograph; 4).

GENERAL

HBW Associates, Inc. Planning aids for a new library building. *Illinois Libraries*. 67(9):794-810; 1985 November.

Presents in outline format the basic elements of planning for a new library building. Covers from the library building project sequence to specifications for purchasing furniture and equipment; components of a building program, selection of the architect, effective space planning, floor-loading factors, lighting, energy management, barrier-free access, and general planning data for shelving and seating.

Lushington, Nolan; Mills, Willis N., Jr. *Libraries designed for users: a planning handbook*. Hamden, CT: Library Professional Publications; 1980. 289p.

Although this book is aimed primarily for mid-sized public library planning, Lushington's experience provides much useful information for the planning of any library. Examines the design process, planning of library buildings, and organizing of books and other media and contains much factual information on size, space, and lighting.

Mason, Ellsworth. *Mason on library buildings*. Metuchen, NJ: Scarecrow; 1980. 333p.

Basic and thorough manual on library planning. Covers preplanning, writing of the library building program, lighting, ventilation systems, and interior design. The second part of the book consists of in-depth reviews for 5 library buildings and evaluations of an additional 100 library buildings. A useful appendix presents a demonstration model program.

Metcalf, Keyes D. *Planning academic and research library buildings*. 2d ed. Leighton, Philip D.; Weber, David C., eds. Chicago: American Library Association; 1986. 630p.

The revised and updated edition to the standard manual on planning academic and research library buildings for twenty years. Its emphasis is on large rather than small libraries. Comprehensive manual that covers the entire range of library building planning, including the planning and construction process, additions and renovations, space requirements, housing collections, lighting, flooring, interior design, and furniture and equipment.

Mount, Ellis, ed. *Planning the special library*. New York: Special Libraries Association; 1972. 122p. (SLA Monograph; 4).

Brief overview of many aspects of planning and equipping the special library. Coverage includes articles on the planning process, space utilization, interior design, floor coverings, furniture, and equipment. Layouts for seven representative special libraries are presented.

Rockwell, Jeanette Sledge; Flegal, Jean E. A checklist with guidelines for library planning. In: Mount, Ellis, ed. *Planning the special library*. New York: Special Libraries Association; 1972; p. 59-79 (SLA Monograph; 4).

Presents an outline with guidelines intended to assist in developing initial planning concepts, formulating a planned program, and organizing the many details involved in library planning. Includes analyzing the library operations, choosing the planning team, preparing the building program, selecting equipment and furniture, doing planning and layout. Specific to the planning of special libraries.

Rovelstad, Howard. Guidelines for planning sci-tech libraries. *Science & Technology Libraries*. 3(4):3-19; 1983 Summer.

Describes a procedure for planning or for doing major renovation of a science-technology library. Discusses initial decisions and preparation, selection of an architect, use of a consultant, and the writing of a program statement that incorporates projections for collections, staff, and services.

Thompson, Godfrey. *Planning and design of library buildings*. 2d ed. London: Architectural Press; 1977. 189p.

Explains basic principles of library planning and design in terms meant for beginners (those planning a new library for the first time). General enough to be applicable to libraries of many types. Topics covered include preparation of the library building program, layout for furniture and equipment, book shelving, furniture, floors, lighting, security and protection, and physical conditions.

PREPLANNING

Hall, Richard B. Communicating with graphics in the library building program. *Illinois Libraries*. 67(9):777-786; 1985 November.

Describes how to use graphics in the building program to enable better communication between the librarian and the architect. Introduces a format to be used for the space requirements component of the building program. Sample data sheet for standardized data collection and diagrams are presented. Notes that an experienced graphics illustrator may be desired.

Holt, Raymond M. Write and use a program: it's the heart of the building project. *Wisconsin Library Bulletin*. 71(5):197-200; 1975 September/October.

Brief article that provides guidance in the preparation of the library building program. Reviews the objectives of a building program, scope and content, space estimating, length and format, and modification.

Lieberfeld, Lawrence. The curious case of the library building. *College and Research Libraries*. 44(4):277-282; 1983 July.

Cites the inconsistency between what is written in the library building program and subsequently built and the actual pattern of use of library buildings. Discussion of reader space and stack space, which constitute 80 to 90 percent of library building space.

LJ annual architectural issue. *Library Journal*. December 1 issue.

Survey of academic and public library buildings completed during the preceding year (July 1 to June 30). Includes both new libraries, additions/renovations, and projects in progress. Facts and figures given for each library include the project cost, gross area, square foot cost, building cost, equipment cost, book capacity, seating capacity, and architect. Useful listing for consideration of potential sites to review or visit.

Mason, Ellsworth. Writing a building program. *Library Journal*. 91(21):5838-5844; 1966 December.

Explains the purpose of a library building program and the elements that should be included. Reviews what should be left to the architect. An augmented and rewritten version of this article appears as Chapter 2 in *Mason on library buildings* (see under **GENERAL**).

Park, Leland. The whys and hows of writing a building program. *Library Scene*. 5(3):2-5; 1975 September.

A practical and concise statement on writing a library building program, specific to a college library but applicable to any library. Explains how a survey of existing facilities, estimate of future needs, and evaluation of each major section of the library make up the building program.

Rohlf, Robert H. Library design: What *not* to do. *American Libraries*. 17(2):100-104; 1986 February.

Reviews some cautions to observe and opportunities to take advantage of during the planning process. Discussion of such problem areas as impractical architectural elements; communication in planning, lighting, furniture, and equipment; and setting of schedules.

PLANNING TEAM: ARCHITECT, CONSULTANT, AND LIBRARIAN

Heimsath, Clovis. How to talk to the architect. *Texas Library Journal*. 53(1):21-23; 1977 Winter.

Discusses the concept of "behavioral architecture" by which the librarian must reconstruct the behavioral patterns within the library building. Communication between the architect and librarian is critical to plan the use of the library in great detail.

Lewis, Myron E.; Nelson, Mark L. How to work with an architect. *Wilson Library Bulletin*. 57(1):44-46; 1982 September.

Two architectural firm partners discuss the communication necessary between the library client and the architect. Addresses the informational requirements of the architect and what the architect is responsible for doing. Notes the importance of being able to fully explain priorities to each other and to accept necessary compromises.

Library buildings consultant list. Chicago: American Library Association, Library Administration and Management Association, Buildings and Equipment Section; latest edition.

Listing of individuals who are active as library building consultants. Gives information for each individual: years as a building consultant, number of recent projects, and special areas of expertise.

Library resources market place. New York: R. R. Bowker; latest edition.

Section on library services includes library architects and library consultants. The selected list for architects consists of the 50 architectural firms that have won an American Institute of Architects/ ALA Library Administration and Management Association library building award during the last 15 years. The list for library consultants lists over 110 companies and individuals and includes a classification by specialty, several of which are applicable to the planning of a special library.

Lushington, Nolan. Designed for users [discussion with architects]. *Wilson Library Bulletin*. 57(2):148-151; 1982 October.

Notes the importance of establishing basic differences between libraries and other buildings the architect may have designed. General consideration of designing for use, collections, services, lighting, bookstacks and weight-bearing, and temperature and environmental control. Discussion is based on public libraries but is useful to any library.

Mason, Ellsworth. Consulting on academic library buildings. *Library Trends*. 28(3):363-380; 1980 Winter.

Discusses the ways in which consulting on library buildings differs from any other kind of library consulting. Advice on whether a consultant is needed, how to select a consultant, the role of the consultant, and consultant fees.

Rohlf, Robert H. The selection of an architect. *Public Libraries*. 21(1):5-8; 1982 Spring.

Details the fundamental criteria for selection of an architect and the process of selection. Presents a general questionnaire to be used for architectural firms under consideration. Emphasizes that the single most crucial criteria in the selection of an architect is the perceived ability for communication. Although aimed at public libraries, is very useful to the selection of an architect for any library.

Zenke, Mary H. Assembling dreams and reality: the job of the library building consultant. *Illinois Libraries*. 67(9):792-794; 1985 November.

Discusses the role of the library building consultant in establishing the priorities of a library building program, other duties of the consultant, finding the right consultant, hiring the consultant, hiring and working with the architect, and the building program statement.

INTERIOR DESIGN AND LAYOUT

American National Standards Institute. *Specifications for making buildings and facilities accessible to and usable by physically handicapped people*. New York: ANSI; 1980; A117.1-1980.

Details the nationally accepted standards for making buildings and facilities accessible to and usable by physically handicapped people. Considerations to be aware of during the design of new buildings and facilities.

Becket, Margaret; Smith, Henry Bradford. Designing a reference station for the information age. *Library Journal*. 111(7):42-46; 1986 April 15.

Discusses the design of a new reference station, both physical and service considerations. Applicable to a new library, renovation, or simple rearrangement of existing furniture, equipment, and services. Considers all aspects of planning, layout, integrating physical layout with new information technology, furniture, and provision of reference service.

Cohen, Aaron; Cohen, Elaine. *Designing and space planning for libraries: a behavioral guide*. New York: R. R. Bowker; 1979. 250p.

This book concentrates on the interior design aspects of library planning with emphasis on the behavioral implications of design. Discussion of behavioral aspects of space; planning and arranging space; furniture and equipment layout; and selection, lighting, color, and signage. Explains calculating space needs, floor loading requirements, power and energy requirements, and bookstack spacing.

Draper, James; Brooks, James. *Interior design for libraries*. Chicago: American Library Association; 1979. 152p.

Explains basic design principles of interior design and their application in general terms. Discusses fundamentals of interior design such as floor plans; wall, floor, and window treatments; and fabric and color and stresses the importance of interior design in the function of the library.

Pierce, William S. *Furnishing the library interior*. New York: Marcel Dekker; 1980. 288p.

General discussion of planning the library interior and the selection, evaluation, and purchase of furniture and equipment. Describes the planning of seating capacity, tables, chairs, types of shelving, nonprint media, and interior appointments. Sample specifications are presented.

Thompson, Godfrey. Furniture and equipment. In: *Manual of library economy*. Lock, R. Northwood, ed. Hamden, CT: Shoe String Press; 1977. p. 135-158.

Describes library furniture and equipment in broad categories by function such as storage/shelving, furniture and fittings, office, and functions unique to libraries. Reviews book shelving sizes, book shelf materials, spacing (common minimum figures are given), compact shelving, storage of other materials, other furnishings, and library decor.

LIGHTING

Ach, William K. Lighting in microtext rooms. *Microform Review*. 14(3):171-173; 1985 Summer.

Emphasizes the dual function of lighting in microform areas, the needs of individual users and the needs of staff (storage and maintenance). Outlines the means of achieving the best lighting through indirect, variable, controlled illumination by use of natural and artificial light.

Illuminating Engineering Society, Subcommittee on Library Lighting of the Committee on Institutions of the IES. Recommended practice of library lighting. *Library Technology Reports*. 1974 July. [Reprinted from: *Journal of the Illuminating Engineering Society*, 3:253-281; 1974.]

Presents the scientific findings and recommendations of the IES in combination with practical application techniques. Discusses the objectives of library lighting, characteristics of light and lighting, lighting design considerations, and lighting system considerations. Gives the current recommended levels of illumination for specified library areas.

Fuhlrott, Rolf. On library lighting. In: Fuhlrott, Rolf; Dewe, Michael, eds. *Library interior layout and design*. London: K. G. Saur; 1982. pp. 106-118 (IFLA Publications; 24).

Observations and proposals for better library lighting. Emphasizes that the lighting concept should be derived from a set of programmed activities, the visual tasks, and biological needs, and that the need for different levels of lighting in different functional areas must be indicated in the building program. Discusses artificial light in relation to visual tasks, and the quality, intensity, costs, and methods of artificial lighting for reading areas and stack areas.

Kaufman, John E., ed. *IES lighting handbook*. 6th ed. New York: Illuminating Engineering Society; 1981. 2 vols.

Basic reference source on all aspects of architectural lighting. The reference volume contains fundamental information on light and vision, measurement of light, color, and sources of light. The applications volume covers lighting design, lighting systems, lighting economics, and specific applications. Gives the current recommended levels of illumination for specified library areas and briefly discusses lighting applications in libraries.

Lushington, Nolan. Designed for users [lighting]. *Wilson Library Bulletin*. 55(8):606-607, 637-638; 1981 April.

Discusses the important part that lighting plays in the design and function of libraries. Briefly reviews different types of lighting, including track lighting.

Lushington, Nolan. Designed for users [lighting]. *Wilson Library Bulletin*. 55(9):684-685, 717; 1981 May.

Reviews the types of lighting sources available. Discusses bookstack lighting and methods of placement and table lighting.

Metcalf, Keyes D. *Library lighting*. Washington, D. C.: Association of Research Libraries; 1970. 99p.

General discussion of lighting and recommendations for artificial lighting in libraries. Describes lighting problems in relation to quality, function, aesthetics, intensity, and costs. Presents consultants' answers to questions, conclusions, and recommendations.

Schleifer, Lawrence M.; Sauter, Steven L. Controlling glare problems in the VDT (video display terminal) work environment. *Library High Tech*. 3(4):21-25; 1985.

Examines the special lighting problems that the VDT (video display terminal) work environment has created. Describes the sources and characteristics of glare, the most common lighting-related problem, and suggests glare control measures through proper lighting system design and adjustment mechanisms.

PHYSICAL ENVIRONMENT
(HEATING, VENTILATING, AND AIR CONDITIONING)

Banks, Paul N. Environmental standards for storage of books and manuscripts. *Library Journal*. 99(2):339-343; 1974 February 1.

Summarizes the factors that might be included in building planning that can influence the preservation, deterioration, and destruction of books. States recommended temperature and humidity standards. Discusses separation of books and people (in so far as possible), ventilation, lighting, shelving, storage of microform, disaster control, and monitoring systems.

Boot, J. Physical conditions and their influence on library layout and design. In: Fuhlrott, Rolf; Dewe, Michael, eds. *Library interior layout and design*. London: K. G. Saur; 1982: pp. 83-93 (IFLA Publications; 24).

Comments on the special environment required by a library so that people feel comfortable and books are preserved. Discusses interior climate and comfort, air temperature, radiation temperature, humidity, and air circulation. Suggests acceptable ranges for temperature.

Koller, Franz. Energy saving in the planning of library buildings. *In*: Fuhlrott, Rolf; Dewe, Michael, eds. *Library interior layout and design*. London: K. G. Saur; 1982 p. 70-82 (IFLA Publications; 24).

Examines energy-conscious design and construction and energy-saving measures applicable during architectural design and to existing buildings. Reviews thermal comfort, the principal factors affecting indoor climate, and heat losses from buildings and how to minimize them.

Lushington, Nolan. Designed for users [heating, ventilation, and air conditioning]. *Wilson Library Bulletin*. 56(5):362-363; 1982 January.

Brief overview of planning for heating, ventilation, and air conditioning (HVAC). Guidelines of things to look for and questions to ask in discussing HVAC with the architect and/or mechanical engineer.

PREPARING FOR AUTOMATION

Brownrigg, Edwin B. Library automation: building and equipment considerations in implementing computer technology. In: *Advances in Library Administration and Organization*; 1982: p. 43-53.

Examines planning and physical considerations in the installation of computer systems in libraries. Presents a sample schedule of events. Physical considerations covered include system layout, floor construction, acoustics, electromagnetic compatibility, temperature, humidity, power requirements, and safety and fire prevention.

Cohen, Elaine; Cohen, Aaron. *Automation, space management, and productivity; a guide for libraries*. New York: R. R. Bowker; 1981. 221p.

Guide to planning for automation in terms of the physical environment of the library in order to maximize productivity. Covers the ideal size of a library, floor plans, proper floor loading, choosing appropriate furnishings, and acoustics. Checklists and worksheets, including typical worksheet to be used to help analyze the components of the total library space.

Corbin, John B. Site preparation. In: *Managing the library automation project*. Phoenix, AZ: Oryx Press; 1985: p. 131-143.

Discusses the elements of physical site preparation that must be completed prior to the installation and operation of an automated system. Addresses the specifications for an in-house computer room, including electrical power, air conditioning/air flow, humidity, flooring, lighting, fire protection, and room monitoring. Also covers terminal work and layouts.

Heathgate, Denis; Stubley, Peter. Building services and environmental needs of information technology in academic libraries. *Program*. 20(1):26-38; 1986 January.

Suggests guidelines for dealing with the impact on the physical environment introduced by information technology. Considers the implications for building services: power, telecommunications, heating and ventilation, lighting, and security and addresses the problems of space layout, design, storage and selection of furniture and equipment.

Physical planning guidelines for housing library systems. *Library Systems Newsletter*. 4(1):4-8; 1984 January.

Details the physical requirements needed to prepare the site to house the installation of an automated system. Specifications are given for space requirements, electrical requirements, power line conditioning, telecommunications requirements, environmental requirements (temperature, humidity, airflow, BTU output, and static protection), terminal requirements, and fire protection requirements.

Roose, Tina. Ergonomics in the library. *Library Journal*. 111(17): 54-55; 1986 October 15.

Addresses some of the ergonomic concerns to be considered in the development of a new electronic library or redesign of an existing library. Issues relating to table and keyboard heights, the importance of adjustability, and lighting are highlighted.

FURNITURE AND EQUIPMENT/MATERIALS SUPPLIERS

Library resources market place. New York: R. R. Bowker; latest edition.

Section on library equipment and materials suppliers. The selected list of over 400 suppliers includes companies that sell the full range of library equipment and materials, as well as those that specialize in items for a special area of library service. Classified by category of equipment or materials.

LJ buyers' guide. *Library Journal.* April 1 issue.

Compilation of companies serving the library community; offering products related to automation and the new information technology as well as traditional products and services. The product directory is arranged by product/service categories. The directory of suppliers lists more than 700 companies with addresses, telephone numbers, and lists of products and services.

Furniture

Eckelman, Carl. A. Evaluating the strength of library chairs and tables. *Library Technology Reports.* 13(4):341-433; 1977 July.

Comprehensive study of the basic design characteristics of tables and chairs to provide the background necessary to make evaluations. Discusses the structural characteristics of table and chair support systems and service loads/forces that act upon tables and chairs in use. Explains the evaluation of library tables and library chairs and presents sample evaluations. Requires a high level of expertise in understanding the report.

Eckelman, Carl A. The use of performance tests and quality-assurance programs in the selection of library chairs. *Library Technology Reports.* 18(5):483-571; 1982 September/October.

Details a performance test method developed for general application to library chairs. Consists of a simplified set of guidelines for evaluation in which basic design characteristics are related to readily definable indicators of quality. Describes the tests, analyzes results, and discusses practical aspects of performance testing and the effective use of such tests.

Farkas, David L. Computer furniture . . . an expert's guide on how to be comfortable at your micro. *Online* 8(3):43-48; 1984 May.

Addresses two physical factors contributing to reported problems associated with microcomputer use: the proper selection and arrangement of computer furniture and proper layout of screen and keyboard. Brief discussion of where and how to buy computer furniture.

Lushington, Nolan. Designed for users [library chairs]. *Wilson Library Bulletin*. 56(10):766-767; 1982 June.

Notes that the choice of the library chair is one of the most important furnishing decisions. Discussions of the variety of purposes for library chairs, ergonomic design, seat heights, and upholstery. Lists five manufacturers of general-purpose library chairs.

Ramsey, Charles G.; Sleeper, Harold R., eds. American Institute of Architects. *Architectural graphic standards*. 7th ed. New York: John Wiley; 1981. 785p.

Comprehensive reference work for architects on graphic standards. Useful in planning layout, estimating space needs, and selecting standard furniture and equipment.

The sourcebook of library technology. [Microform]. Chicago: American Library Association; 1986 [published every two years]. Edited cumulation of *Library Technology Reports*. *Library Technology Reports*. 1966- .

General introductory comments and test reports on various models of chairs and desks, contemporary and conventional, filing/storage cabinets, and other items of library furnishings.

Springer, T. J. Sitting on it—searching for a good chair. *Online*. 8(3):44-45; 1984 May.

Briefly states the principles of sound seating design: anatomical support, work posture support, and stability. Lists the characteristics that a VDT task chair, as foundation of the workstation/office, should exhibit. Applicable to choice of any office function chair.

Shelves and Shelving

Daehn, Ralph M. The measurement and projection of shelf space. *Collection Management*. 4:25-39; 1982 Winter.

Describes the theoretical and practical considerations in the planning and implementation of shelf space surveys. Considers different techniques, measurement, statistical estimates, and statistical projection versus measurement and concludes that shelf space can be estimated accurately enough to be of practical use.

Hanna, Herbert L; Knight, Nancy. Movable compact shelving: a survey of U.S. suppliers and library users. *Library Technology Reports*. 17(1):7-105; 1981 January/February.

Describes the 3 major types of compact shelving: revolving (hinged), sliding drawer-type, and sliding (rolling), and discusses the advantages and disadvantages of compact shelving. Surveys the types of shelving offered by 17 U.S. suppliers. Lists library users with synopsis of users' experiences.

Poole, Frazer G. Selection and evaluation of library bookstacks. *Library Trends*. 13(4):89-103; 1965 April.

Detailed comparison of case-type and bracket-type steel shelving with specifications and descriptions of performance tests for structures and finishes. Discussion of wood shelving.

The sourcebook of library technology. [Microform]. Chicago: American Library Association; 1986 [published every two years]. Edited cumulation of *Library Technology Reports. Library Technology Reports*. 1966- .

Introductory comments on library shelving and test reports on various brands of steel shelving.

Microform Equipment

Microfiche readers for libraries: test reports on 17 models. *Library Technology Reports*. 19(3):223-326; 1983 May/June.

Description, test results, and comments on 17 models that are representative of machines currently manufactured (at time of publication) and designed primarily for enlarging standard microfiche at reductions from 24× to 48×. Includes 3 portable models.

Microfilm readers: test reports on 13 models. *Library Technology Reports*. 17(3):211-281; 1981 May/June.

Description, test results, and comments on 13 models of microfilm readers designed for standard 35mm roll microfilm.

Microform reader-printers for libraries: introductory comments on the LTR test program and test reports on 4 models. *Library Technology Reports*. 17(5):411-482; 1981 September/October.

Descriptions, observations, and comments on four models.

Microform reader-printers for libraries: introductory comments on the LTR testing program and test reports on 10 models. *Library Technology Reports*. 20(6):711-862; 1984 November/December.

Descriptions, observations, and comments on ten models (updated reports for 5 models).

Raikes, Deborah A. Microform storage in libraries. *Library Technology Reports*. 12(3):445-558; 1979 July/August.

Discusses the factors involved in selecting microform storage and defines categories of microform equipment and supplies. Lists manufacturers and distributors.

Photocopy Equipment

Buyers Laboratory, Inc. Photocopiers: introductory comments and test reports on 18 models. *Library Technology Reports*. 20(3);289-416; 1984 May/June.

Explains the plain-paper copying process and types of copiers (low-, medium-, and high-volume). Addresses the question of purchasing, renting, or leasing and calculating cost per copy. Description, test reports, and comments on 18 models.

Buyers Laboratory, Inc. Photocopying equipment: introductory comments and test reports on 15 models. *Library Technology Reports.* 18(1):5-120; 1982 January/February.

Explains copying processes. Discusses the factors to consider in choosing a photocopier and the question of purchase, rent, or lease. Descriptions and test reports on 15 models including assessment of performance and value as compared with similar machines.

TELEFACSIMILE AND TELECOMMUNICATIONS

Boss, Richard W. *Telecommunications for library management.* White Plains, NY: Knowledge Industry Publications; 1985. 180p.

Introduction to telecommunications with emphasis on data communications. Explains telecommunications concepts and application to libraries. Topics covered include telecommunications standards, short-, medium-, and long-distance telecommunications, telecommunications equipment, telecommunications software products, and procurement of telecommunications products. List of suppliers.

High-speed telefacsimile in libraries. *Library Technology Reports.* 19(1):7-111; 1983 January/February.

Reviews facsimile technology, facsimile services, facsimile as a document-delivery system, cost, compatibility, and future directions for telefacsimile. Describes product features with assessment of their applicability to library use and reports on 36 models.

Matthews, Joseph R.; Williams, Joan Frye. Telecommunication technologies for libraries: a basic guide. *Library Technology Reports.* 18(4):335-394; 1983 July/August.

Introduction to the various telecommunication technologies applicable to library and information services for individuals with limited technical background. Explains key technical concepts, identifies available services, and projects developments in the telecommunications field.

Saffafy, William B. Facsimile technology: a guide for computer specialists [with a review of 36 transceivers]. *Computer Equipment Review*. 6(4):3-85; 1985 July.

Reviews facsimile technology. Descriptions and comments on 36 models of facsimile transceivers.

A survey of facsimile equipment. *Library Technology Reports*. 21(2):157-200; 1985 March/April.

Discusses the future of facsimile, determination of the need for facsimile, and selection of a facsimile system. Presents model features and cost comparisons. Reports results of a user survey. List of manufacturers.

Williams, Joan Frye; Matthews, Joseph R. Planning for telecommunications service. *Library Technology Reports*. 19(6);603-641; 1983 November/December.

Guide to identifying and monitoring new cost-effective telecommunications products and services. Explores the implications of deregulation. Discusses identifying a library's telecommunications needs and evaluating the various options in telecommunication technologies.

LIBRARY PROTECTION AND SECURITY

Boss, Richard W. Collection security. *Library Trends*. 33(1): 29-38; 1984 Summer.

Examines responding to the issue of security in a proactive rather than reactive manner and not limiting its approach to physical protections through a number of factors that are within the control of the librarian (policies, procedures). Presents the elements of conducting a security audit in order to determine vulnerability and need for security measures.

Bahr, Alice Harrison. Electronic security for books. *Library Trends*. 33(1): 29-38; 1984 Summer.

Addresses the concerns of effectiveness and affordability. Reviews how current systems work. Discusses determining the need for electronic security for books, protection for other media and computer programs, and other factors to be assessed in determining the present and future role of electronic protection.

Camp, John F. Theft detection systems in libraries. *Library Technology Reports*. 21(2): 121-156; 1985 March/April.

Introduction to electronic security systems in terms of their effectiveness, operation, radio frequency versus electromagnetism, and safety. Evaluations of the only three systems active in the library market: Checkpoints Systems, Inc., Kongo Corporation, and 3M. Discussion and user surveys of the systems offered.

Faulkner-Brown, Harry. Protecting the library against fire: some considerations affecting interior layout and design. In: Fuhlrott, Rolf; Dewe, Michael, eds. *Library interior layout and design*. London: K. G. Saur, 1982: p. 57-69 (IFLA Publications; 24).

Examines the ways in which the safety of library buildings and their contents can influence interior design and layout. Reviews the causes of fire and the protection of library contents against fire by automatic fire detection and extinguishing equipment.

Morris, John. *The library disaster preparedness handbook*. Chicago: American Library Association; 1986. 128p.

Practical guide to protection of buildings, collections, and staff. Coverage includes protection from theft, fire, and flood.

Morris, John. Protecting the library from fire. *Library Trends*. 33(1):49-56; 1984 Summer.

Notes that the primary consideration in planning for fire protection is that 70 percent of library fires are incendiary in origin. Reviews causes of fires and surveys past library fires. Discusses the rationale for automatic sprinkler systems in bookstacks.

CASE EXAMPLES

Ayers, Janet. Facilities for Northwestern University's science-engineering library. *Science & Technology Libraries*. 3(4):77-83; 1983 Summer.

Describes the consolidation of three branch science and technology libraries to form a computerized multi-disciplinary unit, the Seely G. Mudd Library for Science and Engineering. Includes floor plan.

Boyajian, Barbara. Creating a new library facility for Ayerst Laboratories Research, Inc. *Science & Technology Libraries*. 7(1):3-13; 1986 Fall.

Details the special problems relating to long-distance relocation and the establishment of the new library facility. Includes floor plan.

Davitt Maughan, Patricia. Facilities of the Kresge Engineering Library at the University of California, Berkeley. *Science & Technology Libraries*. 3(4):85-93; 1983 Summer.

Describes the history, planning, development, and features of the Kresge Engineering Library. Includes floor plan.

Durkan, Michael J.; Horikawa, Emi K. Facilities of Swarthmore College's Science and engineering library. *Science & Technology Libraries*. 3(4):95-104; 1983 Summer. (See excerpt on p.   .

Describes the various stages of building the Cornell Library of Science and Engineering from estimating space needs to moving into the completed building. Includes floor plan.

Godfrey, Lois Erwin. The libraries of the Los Alamos National Laboratory. *Science & Technology Libraries*. 7(1):57-65; 1986 Fall.

This library is of interest as one of the few sci-tech libraries to rely heavily on a solar heating system (obtaining 94 percent of heat and 70 percent of cooling needs). Features of the facility are described.

Horres, Mary M.; Hitt, Samuel. Renovation and expansion of an academic health sciences library. *Bulletin of the Medical Library Association*. 72(3):301-309; 1984 July.

Describes the planning for the renovation, expansion, and principal design features of the Health Sciences Library at the University of North Carolina at Chapel Hill. An architectural summary gives information on costs and building capacities.

Kotseas, Cosette M. Library facilities for the Riley Stoker Corporation. *Science & Technology Libraries*. 3(4):51-58; 1983 Summer.

Outlines the planning of the Riley Stoker Corporation Library from its development to the present. Includes needs assessment, space allocations, budgetary data, and floor plan.

Kronick, David A. [and others]. The new library building at the University of Texas Health Science Center at San Antonio. *Bulletin of the Medical Library Association*. 73(2):168-175; 1985 April.

Describes the planning process, external features, interior layout, interior design and furnishings, and move to the building for the new University of Texas Health Science Center at San Antonio. Includes floor plan.

McDonald, Isabel G. Remodeled library facilities of the Oregon Regional Primate Research Center. *Science & Technology Libraries*. 3(4):21-30; Summer 1983.

Reports the relocation of the small biomedical library of the Oregon Regional Primate Center to renovated larger quarters. Includes floor plan. (See excerpt on p. 145.)

Pavlin, Stefanie A. [and others]. Design of library facilities for the Ontario Ministry of Transportation and Communications. *Science & Technology Libraries*. 3(4):43-50; 1983 Summer.

Describes the history, planning, design, and move of the Library and Information Centre of the Ontario Ministry of Transportation and Communications. Includes floor plan.

Rupprecht, Ted. Creating new library facilities for the Bendix Advanced Technology Center. *Science & Technology Libraries*. 3(4): 59-75; 1983 Summer.

Describes the formation of the new Bendix Advanced Technology Center Library by selection and move of a core collection from the older library to the new research center. Details maintaining bibliographic control of both collections throughout the move. Includes floor plan.

Ryan, Ken; Galli, Marilyn. Adapting non-library facilities for periodical collections at Brookhaven National Laboratory. *Science & Technology Libraries*. 3(4):31-41; 1983 Summer.

Discusses investigating the use of various recycled non-library facilities as a library annex and several interim solutions to cope with a serious space problem. Details low-cost use of industrial shelving in a former chapel/theatre.

Schulte, Lorraine. A new pharmaceutical company library: the Upjohn Company Corporate Technical Library. *Science & Technology Libraries*. 7(1):15–30; 1986 Fall.

Describes the planning and features of the new Upjohn Company Corporate Technical Library. Highlights the problems of designing a library that would have computer facilities for its users as a major component (over 70 electronic workstations). Includes floor plan. (See excerpt on p. 149.)

Somerville, Arleen N. [and others]. The new Science and Engineering Library at the University of Rochester: blending traditional with electronic. *Science & Technology Libraries*. 7(2):71-93; 1986 Winter.

Describes the planning for a science and engineering library that is to share its building with the computer science departments of the university. Includes floor plan.

Stankus, Tony. The new O'Callahan Science Library at the College of the Holy Cross. *Science & Technology Libraries*. 7(1):45-55; 1986 Fall.

Details the features of the new O'Callahan Science Library at the College of the Holy Cross. Includes floor plan.

Stevens-Rayburn, Sarah. The Space Telescope Institute: launching a new astronomy library. *Science & Technology Libraries*. 7(2):95-103, 1986 Winter.

Describes the planning and development of a small, specialized research library. Includes floor plan.

Swanson, Patricia K. The John Crerar Library of the University of Chicago. *Science & Technology Libraries*. 7(1):31-43; 1986 Fall.

Summarizes the merger of the John Crerar Library with the University of Chicago. Describes the new facility built to house the combined collections as well as problems or merging large collections. Includes floor plan.

INDEX OF BIBLIOGRAPHY CATEGORIES

Architects
Automation Preparation
Case Examples
Consultants
Equipment Suppliers
Furniture
Furniture and Equipment/Materials Suppliers
General
Heating, Ventilating, and Air Conditioning
Interior Design and Layout
Layouts
Library Protection and Security
Lighting
Microform Equipment
Photocopy Equipment

Physical Environment (Heating, Ventilating and Air Conditioning)
Planning Teams: Architect, Consultant, and Librarian
Preparing for Automation
Preplanning
Security
Shelves and Shelving
Telefacsimile and Telecommunications

Appendix A

Library Facilities of the Oregon Regional Primate Research Center[1]

Isabel G. McDonald

BACKGROUND

Nikas[2] has pointed out that "special libraries must adapt themselves to architecture not basically planned for their needs." In 1981, the library of the Oregon Regional Primate Research Center was enlarged and relocated to an area that previously contained its own storage area, the facilities of the Data Processing Department, the Medical Illustration Department, and four administrative offices.

The Oregon Regional Primate Research Center was established in 1960 by the National Institutes of Health as the first of seven centers. The library, which was started in August 1961 as one of the earliest services, had occupied an attractive location in the Administration Building. Its space included 1575 sq. ft. on the upper level (main floor) of this two-story building, plus a small storage area.

The library serves a user population of about 170 employees, of which 35 are scientists. Its facilities are also occasionally used by faculty and students of the nearby Oregon Graduate Center. It presently houses over 14,000 books and periodicals. Its subscriptions number 235. Equipment includes microfilm and microfiche reader/printers and one computer terminal. It has a small collection of

---

Isabel McDonald is the Librarian, Oregon Regional Primate Research Center, 505 N.W. 185th Ave., Beaverton, OR 97006.

historical primatology. The staff consists of 1.0 FTE professionals and 1.2 subprofessionals.

The library had outgrown its shelving and its total space by 1976. By 1981 it had approximately 2000 more volumes than its shelving could accommodate. Various expediences had been used to house this growing collection, but the double shelving of volumes had become critical and dangerous.

In December 1979 the decision was made to relocate the library collection totally on the lower level of the building.

Problems with the existing library were lack of space for collection, insufficient reader space and inadequate work space. There were no offices, no work rooms and no photocopier. The major problem of the new location was lack of shelving and funds to purchase it. Other considerations regarding the new site included 6 pillars, ceilings of various heights, a noisy, hollow-sounding computer floor, water leakage from windows, remote access to a staircase, and distance from the mail room. The only elevator was a slow freight elevator. As with the shelving, there would be no money for additional desks, chairs, filing cabinets, new circulation complex, nor funds to move the collection.

The new storage room (A) was approximately one-third smaller than the old area (Figure A.1). It had two doors, an outside wall, and a pillar. We ignored the inside door at the back of (A). By using the door to the hall, we would have access to the collection during the demolition of walls. In the newly renovated facility, the distance from the circulation desk would be shorter. Because of the physical constraints, we purchased narrow shelving and allowed less than standard width aisles. We selected Aurora doublefaced steel shelving 18 inches wide and planned the aisles at 27 inches. Delivery would take 6 weeks.

THE NEW FACILITY

The new facility (Figure A.2) meets our needs well. We gained the additional shelving so necessary for present needs and enough for 4 to 5 years' growth. We enlarged our size from 1878 sq.ft. to 3250 sq.ft. Although we gained no additional seating, the new arrangement affords readers more working space and privacy. The

FIGURE A.1. Photograph of Library Interior

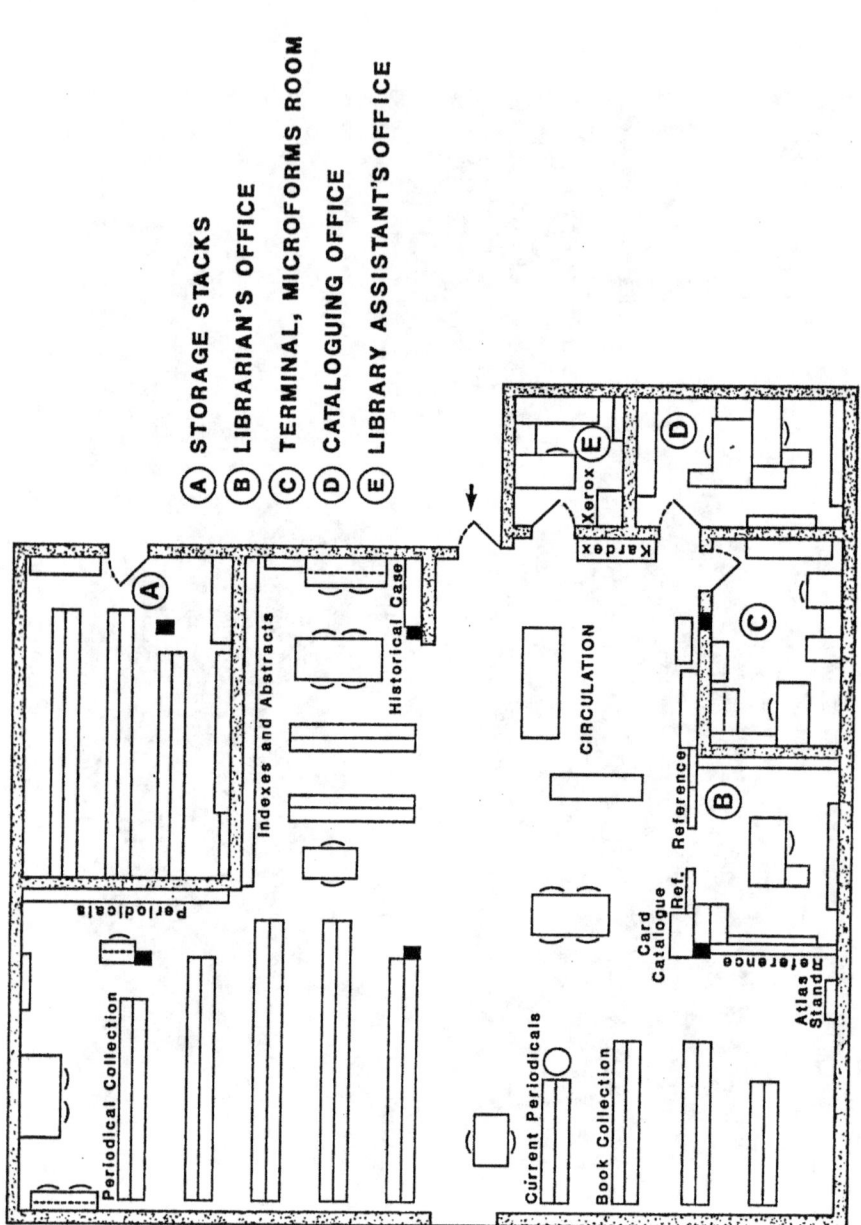

FIGURE A.2. New Floor Plan

library staff now has good working space. The circulation complex designed especially for the original library had to be broken apart. The separate components now frame a circulation "room" that has a feeling of openness but can be reduced in size as space is required for future shelving. Space for additional shelving was designed into the plan (Figure A.1). The new shelving in storage area (A) is a component of Spacesaver movable shelving and can be converted in later years. All staff offices (B), (D), (E) have good visual control and are close to the library entrance.

Room (E) is a small, crowded office (10 feet × 10 feet) which would have been larger were we designing a library. However it functions well. Room (C) with its pillar offered the poorest visual control, and so was planned as the microforms and terminal room. This equipment is centrally located and easily accessible to its many users. Wiring for additional terminals was installed. Indexes and abstracts are much more accessible to the interlibrary loan staff member than they had been in the former library. This corner of the library is one of the most attractive areas of the library. The card catalog was placed near the book collection for the convenience of users and library staff.

The walls, painted either blond yellow or antique white, give a sunny appearance at all times despite the small windows 7 feet 3 inches above the floor. An outside ledge extending beyond the tops of the windows seems to buffer the light so that the quality is pleasant and even. A glass door on an outside wall located near the current periodicals also provides light. The main door to the library is glass with a wooden frame.

The minor losses are the convenient access to the mail room and a beautiful view. The gains are multitudinous. The library staff is pleased with the new library facility and its layout. After 24 months we have made few changes. The total appearance is much more attractive than we envisioned. The lighting is excellent. We prefer it to the radiation experienced in the original library with its two outside walls of glass. The heating seems better regulated and is more comfortable. Our additional phone on the pillar is an extra convenience for the user as well as any staff member working in the periodicals area.

The Center's administration gave great support to the library during and after its relocation. The library acquired a photocopier from the upper level, a number of wooden bookcases from previous tenants, some desks and cabinets, and some large handsome plants that have thrived in the new location.

We believe that we have made significant improvements to our library facility with extremely limited funds.

TABLE A.1. Library Statistics

Gross area	3,259 sq. ft.
Staff size	
Professional	1 FTE
Nonprofessional	1.2 FTE
Seating for users	17
Potential professional patrons	235
Collection size	
Books and bound serials	17,000
Current periodical subscriptions	
(paid and gift)	200
Date of completion	June 1981
Special equipment	photocopier
	microfiche reader-printer
	microfilm reader
	microfiche readers (2)
	OCLC M300 workstation, plus printer

REFERENCES

1. McDonald, Isabel G. Remodelled library facilities of the Oregon Regional Primate Research Center. *Science & Technology Libraries*. 3(4):21-30; 1983 Summer.

2. Nikas, Mary. Interior design: beauty is our excuse. In: *Planning the special library*. Ellis Mount, ed. New York: Special Libraries Association; 1972: p. 22.

Appendix B

The Upjohn Company Corporate Technical Library[1]

Lorraine Schulte

The Upjohn Company is a worldwide, research-based manufacturer and marketer of pharmaceuticals, health services, seeds, and agricultural specialties with corporate headquarters in Kalamazoo, Michigan. There are 22,000 Upjohn employees worldwide, approximately 8000 in the Kalamazoo area, including 1200 research division personnel. Library information services are provided by the Corporate Technical Library, the Business Library and a Medical Information Unit that serves the medical division and provides product information support to the company and the consumer. A number of unit (departmental) collections in Kalamazoo and overseas subsidiary collections and information services form an Upjohn library network. The Corporate Technical Library (CTL) has a staff of 40, including 19 library information professionals and 21 office staff. The mission of the library is to provide systems, services, and expertise for selecting, managing, and disseminating technical information, both public and corporate, to Upjohn technical and management personnel to support the development of the pharmaceutical and agricultural businesses.

LIBRARY SERVICES AND COLLECTIONS

In addition to technical and information services common to most libraries, the library has responsibility for several corporate infor-

---

Lorraine Schulte is Director, Corporate Technical Library, Upjohn Company, 7171 Portage Road, Kalamazoo, MI 49001.

mation systems and for research records management. Library staff create and maintain the corporate Product Information Retrieval System Upjohn (PIRSU) database and a published product literature archive. PIRSU can be searched online from any Upjohn location worldwide. A parallel online information system for internal proprietary literature is also created and maintained by library staff. The records management responsibility includes central filing and management of research records, filing policies and procedures, and a uniform subject classification system for paper, microfilm, and electronic filing media.

The library is open 24 hours for company walk-in users, but is staffed only for the normal 8-hour day. A large portion of the client population, especially those off-site and overseas, access library services through telephone, teletype, paper mail and electronic mail. Library information specialists and information scientists with degrees in both chemical or biological sciences and library/information science provide information services through direct participation on drug development teams as well as on demand. Reference services, literature search services, current literature alerting and special current alerting publications based in PIRSU and proprietary literature database updates are among the services offered. User education programs include an annual series of library seminars, tours, and orientations for individuals or groups; instruction for specific subject area resources; and end-user online search training for the PIRSU product literature system and other commercially available databases.

All technical services operations—acquisitions, periodicals control, bindery, and cataloging—are supported by the LIS (Library Information System) integrated library automation system. The Corporate Technical Library provides periodical subscription and bindery services for clients as well as for the library collection, and it is the central cataloging unit for all Upjohn libraries and unit collections. A corporate online catalog is supported by LIS, as is automated circulation of library materials. Document delivery services are also provided.

The size of the collection, especially the retention of bound periodicals (43,000 volumes), is a reflection of the geographic location of the library and the need to provide rapid turnaround on document requests. There are no major nearby medical, scientific, or technical library resources for local document delivery backup. For a special library devoted primarily to current research, the Corporate Technical Library must therefore keep a rather large number of older periodicals. Even though space for library materials is expensive, some of this cost is traded off against the ability to retrieve needed documents within 24 hours.

Special attention to collection control, not just development, is critical in this environment. The collection is reviewed annually for retention and discard decisions, and there is an active program to convert medium-use periodicals to 16 mm microfilm cartridges. These are interfiled alphabetically in the bound journal stacks. Product literature, technical reports, patents, and some periodical indexes are also kept on 16 mm microfilm cartridges. A weekly library publication announces additions to the CTL and the decentralized unit collection, new Upjohn-authored publications and patents, and videotapes of in-house lectures and presentations from invited speakers.

Computer and computer-associated equipment in support of library systems and services is substantial, and during the planning process considerable attention was given to handling this equipment. There are over 70 electronic workstations in the library, not including Online Training Center equipment. If one were to count the number of associated devices such as printers, modems, graphic tablets, barcode readers, etc., the electronic equipment inventory numbers in excess of 180 items. Major systems components include: 8 stations linked to a DEC WS248 processor for literature search downloading and editing; 16 terminals hardwired to the research divisions' mainframe access electronic mail, SAS-based library record keeping files, proprietary literature databases, and the STAIRS-based Upjohn Storage and Retrieval Technology (UPSTART) for personal bibliographic file management. The integrated library automation system, LIS (Library Information System) runs on a DEC PDP 11/44 and includes 26 stations in the Corporate Technical Library plus 8 stations at decentralized Upjohn library and unit collection locations.

PLANNING THE NEW FACILITY

The new Corporate Technical Library facility was intended to provide adequate space for library clients and staff and to allow collection growth for ten years. A major focus of planning for the new facility was the need to support a rapidly developing and changing electronic library. Functional departmental relationships that were lost when various library departments moved to other research site locations were to be reestablished. Improvements in access to the collection were expected through integration of all collections in one location. Control of the collection was also a major goal since decentralized and unstaffed collection locations, multiple exits that by-passed the circulation desk in the old library, and round-the-clock library hours contributed to loss of materials.

Planning began in earnest in early 1983 for a new seven-story multifunction research building. Although primarily for laboratories and animal rooms, it included a second floor allocated for a new technical library. A library program of requirements, originally prepared in 1979, was revised and updated. The program statement contained information on the library's institutional environment, its mission, client population, collections, services, philosophy, space needs, and plans for the future. The program was a major tool for communicating the library's goals to the library design consultant, architects, and other planners. Construction of the multifunction research building was to be carried out by an architectural and construction firm that had been involved in previous Upjohn research projects.

A library planning team was formed including the library director, two additional library staff, representatives from Upjohn Engineering, Pharmaceutical Research and Development Facilities Planning, Corporate Office Planning Services, and a contract architect. Electrical lighting and other specialty engineers, the library design consultant, and other library staff participated on the team as needed. The library staff also worked independently with the library design consultant, who developed a number of schematics for alternative layouts. All library staff were involved in selection of the schematic of choice, and from that scheme a detailed plan was produced by the library consultant. The schematics and early layout design was also shared with library clients to solicit input. The final plan was reviewed and approved by the library planning team, and construction drawings were produced by the building contractor.

Although the library was to occupy the entire 30,000 gross square feet on the second floor of the new facility, a higher percentage (more than 15 percent) than would be expected in an office building of that size, was not usable. Because construction had to accommodate laboratories and animal facilities, such things as multiple animal elevators, in addition to passenger and freight elevators, took away much usable space.

The most significant loss of usable space was from the utility shafts, which ran in two rows along the entire 300-foot north-south length of the building. These shafts were very large, approximately 5×10 feet, to accommodate special laboratory chemical, air, and water handling needs. The shafts presented no particular problem to a modular laboratory design, but presented a severe problem in creating a visually open and yet integrated library facility. The problem was solved quite effectively by incorporating these utility shafts into the office areas, and then building closets, photocopy and microfilm equipment into the alcoves created by the spaces between them, essentially hiding them.

This approach to hiding the shafts worked best if the majority of library staff offices were located in the interior of the library. The north-south window walls could then be incorporated as part of the open area of the library where user seating and materials would be located. Although moving offices into the interior of the floor was a difficult decision for the staff to make, the superiority of this arrangement architecturally, functionally, and for the overall appearance of the library was clear to everyone.

THE NEW LIBRARY

Construction was begun in May of 1982 and the new library opened in April of 1984. Moving was accomplished in a four-day period, spanning a weekend, with the assistance of a library moving firm and many staff. Moving offices and collections from six locations, and alphabetically integrating bound periodicals from two locations presented special challenges, but there were no major moving problems.

Library materials capacity in the new facility is approximately 86,000 volumes. Although reference collection shelving is essentially filled to capacity, the collection is expected to remain stable at about 2000 volumes. Reference collection expansion can be accommodated in the index and abstract area, if necessary. The area with relatively little growth space and the greatest capacity for growth is the bound journal area. To keep the library in this space for even ten years requires removal of about 300 linear feet of bound periodicals per year for each of ten years of post-occupancy, either by discarding volumes or by microfilm conversion. To make reading and producing copies from the growing microfilm collection convenient, microfilm reader-printers are distributed throughout the bound journal stacks along with photocopy equipment.

Collections of scientific indexes, patents, product literature, and technical reports on 16-mm microfilm are housed centrally in a media area with reader-printers and other stations for slide/tape programs, videocassettes, etc. The library's small collection of commercially available educational media is augmented by a large collection of videocassette recordings of weekly in-house lectures and presentations by visiting scientists. These are kept at the nearby circulation desk.

The reference (information) desk was placed near the main center aisle, directly facing entering visitors. The desk was designed to hold two to three computer terminals and, when necessary, two staff. The computer equipment can be placed in any location on the desk and easily changed because of a wiring raceway built along the inside edge of the facing of the desk. The circulation desk was designed to accommodate a book card-based circulation for one year post-occupancy and then LIS terminals for automated circulation. The circulation desk is just to the left as you enter the library. A Checkmate security system unit flanks the entry and serves as a reminder to appropriately charge library materials.

The carpet chosen for the library includes both carpet tiles and broadloom. Taupe carpet tiles form the matrix in which islands of dark brown carpet tiles define seating area and islands of deep royal blue broadloom define all stack areas. The sides and bases of all stacks are custom-colored blue to match the broadloom on which they rest; remaining shelves are beige. All of the library furnishings in the public areas are finished in light oak with plum and blue upholstery accents.

Staff offices are by corporate policy open-landscape plan offices. This design was followed in the new Corporate Technical Library with few exceptions. Attention was given to long-term needs for equipment and the possibility of staff turnover so that current technology and individual preference did not inhibit a good, flexible overall design. The modular office furniture with interchangeable, attached work surfaces and storage units added a lot of flexibility. Standard clerical office sizes had to be stretched somewhat to include in some cases as many as three different video display terminal workstations. In some processing areas, additional counters were planned near individual offices, and shared workstation areas (e.g., OCLC) were also developed. Fabric panels and chair upholstery for the open-plan offices were either oatmeal with plum accents or oatmeal with blue accents. Technical Services' open-plan offices were left more accessible to the central public area, the reference desk and the User Search Lab.

The computer room houses the DEC, PDP 11/44 for the Library Information System; a DEC WS 248 system for online searching, downloading, and formatting; modems and the master cable patch panel; and various printers—a research mainframe printer, a high-speed printer on a leased line direct to a commercial database vendor, and a letter-quality printer. The computer room required a raised floor to accommodate wiring associated with this equipment.

SPECIAL FEATURES

The current journal shelving was custom designed to allow for storage of multiple issues stacked with covers facing outward on shelves that recline at a 5 degree angle. The issues are held in place by a clear plastic bookend, the base of which fits into a slot between the back and the bottom portion of the shelf. This type of shelving permits the journal covers themselves to serve as titles, eliminating the need to add, change, and delete shelf label titles as the collection grows and changes. Individual shelf ends were also eliminated between each 3-foot section of shelving, providing 12 linear feet of continuous shelf space per row. The current journal shelving can accommodate between 1200 and 1500 titles, depending on how closely the titles are packed in each 12-foot row.

Individual study carrels were designed so that the carrel wall on the window side was reduced to only a 2-inch height. This allowed for both a visually open appearance to the library and individual reader enjoyment. In addition to the 12 audiovisual stations centralized in the media area, 4 special purpose microfilm reader-printer carrels were designed for the bound journal stacks. A number of the individual study carrels were also wired to accommodate electronic equipment, including terminals for the online catalog in each of the 3 major stack areas, books, and bound journals north and bound journals south (see the layout in Figure B.1.)

File cabinets housing a large collection of internal reports were used to create a partition for the circulation office area, placed back-to-back with a row of supply cabinets. An H-shaped arrangement of light oak, wooden end panels was made to surround the horizontal files and the supply cabinets, with a partition between them. The partition surface visible above the file cabinets (on back of the supply cabinets) was covered with the same fabric used on open landscape office partitions. The unit has created effective office privacy without obstructing the view past the circulation desk to the far end of the library where monographs are shelved.

Each of the Information Services staff offices houses a computer terminal for literature searching and downloading. Two office spaces in this area house shared special-use terminals (graphics and mainframe). A central collection of search stations was also made available in a User Search Lab: a research computer mainframe terminal; TTY terminal, a personal computer; two chemical graphics stations, one DEC retrographics terminal, and an IBM PC/AT for both in-house and commercially available chemical graphics systems. Although a majority of the research staff have computer equipment in their offices and laboratories, certain conditions such as increases in the end-user searchers, the limited numbers of special-purpose graphics terminals in offices, and the convenience of accessing computer data files in the library, suggested the need for

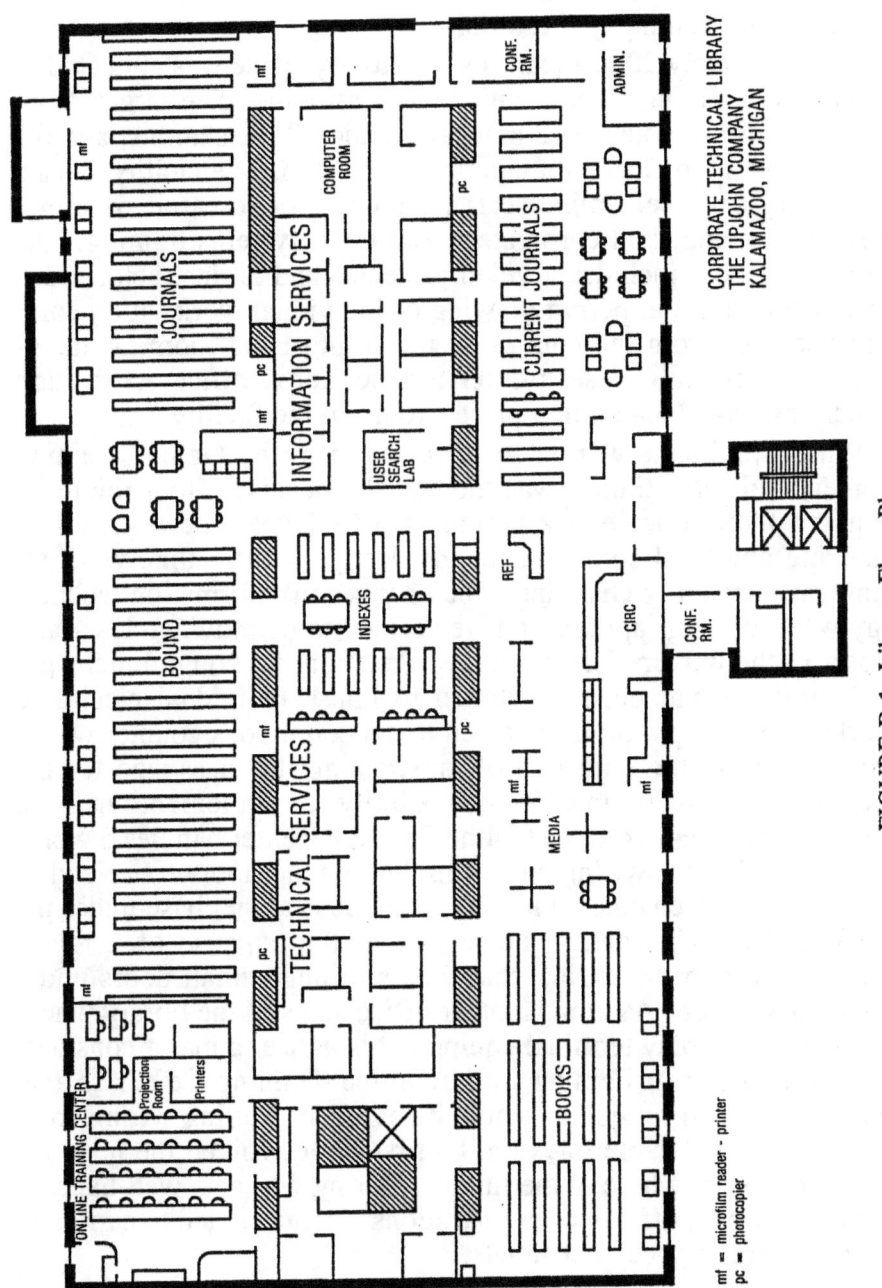

FIGURE B.1. Library Floor Plan

this kind of facility. The User Search Lab is also used for one-on-one end-user training and tutorials.

Approximately 2000 square feet of library space was allocated to an Online Training Center with two classrooms. The larger room currently accommodates 12 mainframe and 12 PC stations, and the smaller room 5 office-automation workstations. The facility is used for library end-user online search training, for research computer systems training, and corporate information systems training. The large classroom includes a video projector and an instructor video access network that permit viewing of individual workstation computer screens from the console at the front of the room. A mainframe printer and a laser printer for the Xerox office automation system are also located in a printer room in the facility.

Wiring problems were a major concern in the Online Training Center, and for a time it was thought that a raised floor might be required there too. Over a period of 3 to 4 years between initial planning and final construction, the design of the online workstation was constantly changing. The changes in information technology were moving rapidly, and we seemed to be moving closer and closer to the universal electronic workstation. Although much special furniture had been developed to house individual electronic workstation setups, it was decided that a continuous counter would best help meet the objective of maximizing the class size for the facility and allowing maximum flexibility for equipment changes. Each 28-foot counter in the Online Training Center handles 6 workstations. All of the wiring comes up through the floor on one end of the room and is channeled into a continuous cabinet base under the workstations. This design helped avoid the expense of a raised floor. Access to the wiring channels is through small doors under each workstation. As in most other office areas of the library where much video display terminal equipment is in use, a major consideration was given in lighting in the Online Training Center so that screen glare and reflection would be avoided. Pulling wiring from ceiling-mounted cable trays on the first floor avoided the need for power poles anywhere in the library. Wiring was also well handled in the open-plan offices where partitions were designed to carry and conceal wire in special channels.

In accordance with a company policy of supporting local and

regional art, a variety of sculptures, tapestries, paintings, and limited edition prints were purchased for the library.

OUTCOME

The overall results were extremely pleasing visually and a success functionally. The project was successful in meeting its primary objectives of providing adequate user and staff space, collection space, and electronic library facilities. The reaction from clients and upper management has been overwhelmingly positive. (See Figure B.2.)

Problems with the new facility were limited. A significant staff adjustment to open-plan offices was required, especially because white noise originally planned for the library floor had been eliminated as an economy measure. Each staff member has an individual office with visual and psychological privacy, but normal office conversation and telephone calls can be overheard many offices away. Careful attention to modulating conversation volume and just plain learning to live with it has helped. The Upjohn telephone system permits variable ring tone and ring patterning that help distinguish multidepartmental calls within large office space.

There was some concern with lighting in the public reception areas and over the study carrels. Metal halide downlights created a very dramatic effect in these areas, but their localized intensity created glare interrupted by dark spots and shadows over the circulation and reference desks. The downlights in these areas were exchanged for fluorescent lighting with parabolic lenses. All offices have finished ceilings with fluorescent lights and parabolic lenses. Unfinished, exposed ceilings in the bound journal and book stack areas were painted black and equipped with fluorescent lighting (with light modulating Fresnel lenses) running perpendicular to the shelving at stack top height. The lighting defines the effective ceiling height in these stack areas.

The microfilm carrels custom designed for the large microfilm reader-printers proved somewhat bulky and needed modification for convenient operation of the equipment. Modifications to the online catalog unit were also made to improve wire handling, essentially hiding the traverse of wires from the counter to the floor.

FIGURE B.2. Photograph of Library Interior

Other recent additions have been a computer room security system requiring an authorized I.D. badge for access after hours. A special alarm system monitoring temperature and humidity was also installed. The room has its own self-contained air cooling system.

Closets for storage and coats were designed into the utility shaft alcoves and at other locations, but storage space is still tight. It seems almost impossible to plan too much storage or unplanned space; we wish we had a bit more. There was a limit on the space we could plan for staff expansion within the allotted space; addition of more than two new staff will surely send us to the shelf areas for space to convert to additional offices. This might also help push the adoption of alternative storage media, such as optical disc, or access to electronic journals.

Two years of occupancy have not uncovered any major problems or concerns about what might have been. The library appears to be wearing rather well, already accommodating equipment, office, and staffing changes. Continued attention to consistency in choice of colors and design for library furnishings, accessories, signage, etc., will aid in keeping the facility looking new for many years to come.

TABLE B.1. Library Statistics (1987)

Gross area	30,000 sq. ft.
Net usable space	25,000 sq. ft.
Date of completion	April 1984
Staff	
Professional	19
Nonprofessional	21
Employees served at location	8,000
Seating	
Carrels	27
Index/abstract stations	18
Av/microfilm stations	20
Table seats	40
Lounge chairs	18

Collection size	Collection	Capacity
Books	15,000	24,000
Reference collection	2,000	2,000
Indexes/abstracts	3,200	6,600
Bound journal volumes	43,000	53,000
Current monographic serials	400	53,000
Current periodical subscriptions	1,200	1,500

Services
Circulation	20,000
Document delivery requests	54,000
Current alerting profiles	1,000
Literature search requests	3,600

Equipment
LIS integrated library system terminals	26
Research computer mainframe terminals	16
OCLC stations	3
FAXON datalinx terminals	4
Downloading and data capture stations	8
Chemical structure search stations	3
Xerox word-processing stations	5
General purpose search terminals	8

REFERENCE

1. Schulte, Lorraine. A new pharmaceutical library: The Upjohn Company Corporate Technical Library. *Science & Technology Libraries*. 7(1): 15-29; 1986 Fall.

Appendix C

Swarthmore College's Science and Engineering Library[1]

Michael J. Durkan
Emi K. Horikawa

BACKGROUND

Swarthmore College was founded in 1864 by members of the Society of Friends as a coeducational institution. It is situated in the borough of Swarthmore on some 300 acres of rolling, wooded land about fifteen miles to the southeast of Philadelphia.

The College Libraries consist of the following units: McCabe Library (the general collection), the Cornell Library of Science and Engineering, the Underhill Music Library, the Friends Historical Library (a collection of Quaker materials) and the Peace Collection. The latter two are housed within the McCabe Library. Together they amount to some 600,000 volumes and some 2800 periodical subscriptions. The newest unit is the Cornell Library of Science and Engineering, dedicated in December 1982 and housing some 60,000 volumes and 830 periodical subscriptions.

The early history of library accommodation for Science and Engineering at Swarthmore College is similar to that of most institutions. Small departmental collections were established in each departmental office. Borrowing and use were pretty much left to the individual faculty member, student use was limited. These satellite libraries were maintained by a librarian from the main college library on a weekly basis. In 1959 a new building was provided to

---

Michael J. Durkan is College Librarian, Swarthmore College, Swarthmore, PA 19081. Emi K. Horikawa is Science Librarian at Swarthmore College.

house the departments of Chemistry, Mathematics and Physics. It was felt that this would be a good time to gather together the library materials for these departments as well as for Engineering and house them in an area developed especially for their use. The library was not represented on the planning committee and had minimal input on space and arrangement. The space devoted to the library was a rectangular room of about 5000 square feet which included a small office for the librarian. The librarian with supporting staff of 1.5 people and student assistants was responsible for the administration of the DuPont Science Library as well as for the departmental collections housed in the departments of Astronomy and Biology which were still operating as departmental libraries.

By the end of ten years, space in the DuPont Library was filled to capacity. The main problem was how to exist and provide service in the face of a growing collection with no provision for expansion. Storage was the immediate answer. Back files of certain periodicals were sent to be housed in the Central Library; some monographs were stored in an area allocated to the Science Library by the department of Chemistry. Weeding was a continuing activity. These were however only stop-gap measures. It was clear that additional space was needed for books, for readers and for staff.

By January 1980, a committee with representation from the library, the college administration and the science faculty, was established to choose the architect for the project. By January 1981, the Philadelphia firm H2L2 Architects/Planners had been designated as the architects of the proposed new building. The Paul Restall Company of Swarthmore was chosen as the construction company for the facility, which would be ready for use by September 1982.

The program presented to the architects called for a building that would house library materials and make them readily available to users. Other expectations were as follows: the new library would be flexible, friendly, warm and pleasant; it would be a live, vital place, capable of growth and change; special emphasis would be placed on the library as an active participant in the teaching and learning program; since most of the materials would be open to readers, the design would provide the greatest possible access to them; there would be high use of the building for study since most of the students, the prime users, would be living on campus. Special attention would be paid to periodicals—both for storage and display; to microforms; and to the increasing use of technology encompassing on-line retrieval, together with other innovations. Both individual and group seating and lounge areas would be provided; lighting, environmental controls and floor coverings also were specified. The space requirements for each area and activity were specified in detail, accompanied by a text indicating its special needs and its particular function. The architects were also provided with check lists of items of special concern that would not be covered in the program statements: telephones, signs, clocks, bookdrop, keys, electrical outlets, etc. The final document provided was a "space requirements summary" listing the square footage for each area with an overall total of 13,210 square feet.

PLANNING

Once the architectural firm had been chosen, a series of weekly meetings was initiated—attended by the architects, the college engineer, the college librarian and the science librarian. A three-story building was chosen so as to minimize the building footprint on this particular site. The details were worked out swiftly and efficiently, the library presenting its needs and requirements, the architects incorporating them in their planning, and the college engineer determining their feasibility and conformity with local ordinances.

During this process, advice was continually sought from all constituencies through correspondence and meetings with various groups of faculty, students, administration, and library staff. The building folder from the American Library Association was obtained on interlibrary loan; much advice, solicited and otherwise, was received. The staff of the College Library provided much valuable information. Their specific suggestions included: carpeted floors for comfort and quiet; operable windows; drains for floors of rest rooms; overhead carrel lighting separate from individual carrel lights; a vestibule to serve as a weather-lock and with a recessed mat to remove outside snow and grime before entering; lockable book drop and special shelving. Based as they were on practical experience, their opinions were especially useful and were invariably followed in detail.

Recognizing that the prime users would be students and faculty, we at every stage, both formally and informally, solicited their opinions. Both constituencies were represented on the initial planning committee and were brought in again at the various stages of development, e.g., interior decoration and furniture selection. Student concerns were also voiced frequently in informal conversations at the circulation desk and at the study tables in the DuPont Library. Some were especially useful, others not so — we listened to them all and showed the students we welcomed their suggestions.

During construction, as soon as the exterior has been completed and when the interior arrangement is in recognizable shape, it is important that the librarian should visit the site frequently. Since the librarian knows the specific requirements; she or he can keep an eye out to make sure that the specifications are observed in all detail and to see that they are corrected if they vary. We found that this was best achieved by contacting the college engineer and having him make representations to the architects or to the construction firm. In some cases the architect was approached directly by the librarian. There were many details that were rectified at that stage that would have been next to impossible to take care of in the completed building.

COMPLETED BUILDING

The structure is flat slab floors supported by round concrete columns and 8-inch CMU bearing walls. Interior partitions are of exposed concrete block and drywall. There are aluminum curtain walls at front and back. The floor coverings are of carpet and ceramic tile. A rich magenta color was chosen for the carpet to contrast with the grey concrete interiors, while lounge furniture is in shades of purple, green and red. The wooden furniture (current periodical shelving, card catalog, carrels, chairs) is of light oak. Some of the furniture from the DuPont Library was refinished for use in the new building, as was the metal shelving for the bound periodicals on the upper level. Ceilings are exposed on the lower and main levels, leaving the air ducts and other conduits in full view. The air ducts are painted in a shade of very light purple to harmonize with the magenta carpet. The library has net area of 16,770 sq. ft., with a seating capacity of 178 and a volume capacity of 120,000 volumes.

The three-level design of the building places current periodicals, reference, card catalog and administration on the entry level, sandwiched between bound periodicals and microforms on the upper level and monographs on the lower level. As can be seen from Figure C.1, on the first floor the current periodicals surround an area of comfortable lounge seating overlooking the lower level and with an unobstructed view to the woods outside. Nearby is the reference desk with an online search terminal, the card catalog leading to the reference area with indexes and abstracts, with study and consultation tables along the front wall. To the left as you enter is the staff and administrative area with the circulation desk (concrete block with oak top) extending outwards. Behind the circulation desk along the wall are the staff lounge, staff office, librarian's office and seminar room. The staff area has a view of the circulation desk, which can be closed off as desired. Doors open to the public area, giving a sense of closeness and approachability to library users. The seminar room with blackboards and projection screen is fitted for computer terminals. It was designed for small gatherings of about ten people and is already in much demand. The ceramic tile floor surrounds this whole area and acts as a pathway to the top of the stairs leading to the lower level. A coffee corner for student and faculty use is located immediately to the left as you enter the library. In it are located a counter, sink, hot plate and cabinets. Seating from the old Biology Library has been placed in this tiled area—hot beverages are forbidden outside of this location. This student-run service is much appreciated and is regarded as a special privilege. Close to the coffee corner is the photocopy machine placed within an area designed to minimize noise, with counter space and storage for supplies.

A broad carpeted staircase leads to the lower level, which houses the monograph collection arranged in L.C. class order. (See Figure C.2.) The stair leads to a lounge area with a large semicircular window looking out on the woods. Study space in this level is devoted mostly to large study tables with some individual carrels tucked under the stairway. The Sigma Xi Room, a seminar room fitted by the local chapter, is located on this floor together with two typing rooms and two rooms to serve the handicapped. Entrance to the top level is by either of two stairwells on the entrance level. This is the largest of the three floors with individual carrels along two sides. Bound periodicals, arranged alphabetically by title, are

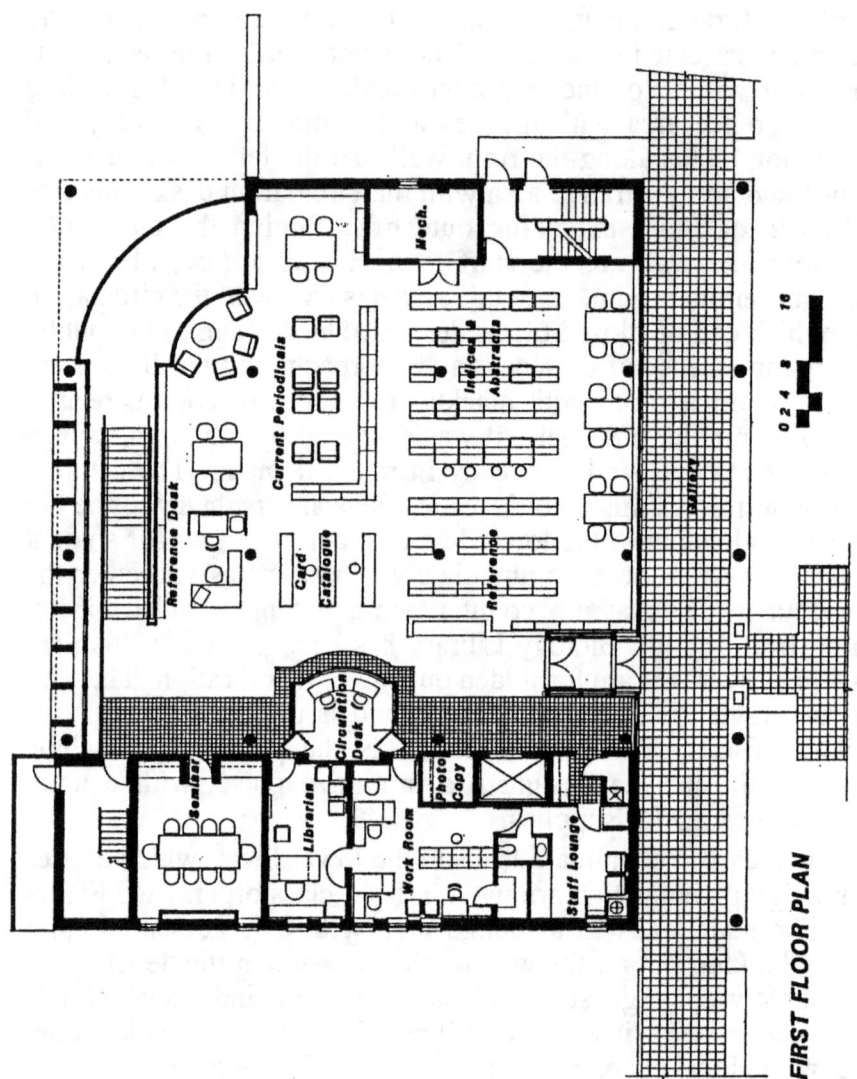

FIGURE C.1. Swarthmore College's Science and Engineering Library

FIGURE C.2. Swarthmore College's Science and Engineering Library (Photograph by Bob Wood)

shelved here. The microforms room is located at one end adjacent to three lockable study carrels. Group study seating, a lounge area (with a student-run, uncataloged science fiction collection) and public restrooms complete the arrangements on this level. The clerestory at the front of the building brings much natural light onto this floor, giving it an airy feeling, emphasized by the aluminum ribbed ceiling which extends throughout the entire clerestory both inside and out. This is the place for quiet, concentrated study and research in contrast to the varying busyness of the other two floors.

As a working library the building is functional and pleasant. The general layout seems to work well — the arrangement of functions and of the collection is clear, direct and easily understood. The small library atmosphere combined with the spacious accommodations provides a pleasing environment for study, research and browsing. The use of some furnishings from the old library gives a sense of continuity and the presence of old friends. The division by floors has underlined the differences in the study habits of the students. Those who cannot work except in busy surroundings will usually be found on the entrance or lower levels, others who require absolute calm and quiet will opt for the carrels and tables on the top level.

Since the Library seeks to be an active partner in teaching and learning, the building in its openness and in its accommodation to students provides the climate for learning. The staff, the book collection, online search facilities, microforms, and catalogs are all easily accessible. The spirit of inquiry is facilitated by the availability of the services and materials housed in the building. On all floors in the study carrels (both locked and open), in the seminar rooms and in the microforms room, provision has been made for the addition of computer terminals. Seventeen are currently available for student use — seven of which are online with the college's Prime mainframe — and ten MacIntoshes.

Zoned climate controls are used, allowing for the minimum of energy to be used especially during vacation periods. There is a solar domestic hot water system. Much natural light comes into the building on all levels. Where this is not sufficient, individual range and carrel lights also control energy use.

The building is set into a bank overlooking the Crum Woods, an area of fine natural, unspoiled beauty. Staff, students and faculty are very happy with the facility and show their pleasure by their frequent use of it.

TABLE C.1. Library Statistics (1987)

Gross area	20,230 sq. ft.
Staff size	
Professional	1
Nonprofessional	1.5
Seating for users	141
Students and faculty served	1,500
Collection size	
Books	29,500
Periodicals (bound & microforms)	26,000
Current periodical subscriptions	640
Date of completion	August 1982
Special equipment	microfilm reader/printer, computer terminals, photocopier

REFERENCE

1. Durkan, Michael J.; Horikawa, Emi K. Facilities of Swarthmore College's Science and Engineering Library. *Science & Technology Libraries*. 3(4): 95-104; 1983 Summer.

Appendix D

Paul, Weiss, Rifkind, Wharton & Garrison Library

Deborah S. Panella

The Paul, Weiss, Rifkind, Wharton & Garrison Library serves the law firm's 335 lawyers and 70 paralegals. The firm's legal departments include corporate, litigation, tax, real estate, personal representation, entertainment, and international practice. The library is staffed by 36 people, 11 of whom hold an MLS. The pace is hectic; the reference staff now handles over 700 requests per week.

The collection is primarily a law collection, although we do have many general reference and business titles. The current volume count is approximately 75,000, which includes 1200 periodical titles and the microforms collection. The library contains 18,500 linear feet of shelving, which we expect will eventually hold 85,000 volumes.

Although we would have preferred the library to be consolidated into one location, there are departmental libraries scattered on 7 of the firm's 12 floors. The breakdown per location is as follows:

LIBRARY	Linear Feet	Square Feet
Main Library	12,000	9,835
Corporate Library	1,300	1,390
Tax Library	1,000	820
Real Estate Library	300	415
Personal Representation Library	150	250
Library Technical Services	100	3,065

Deborah S. Panella is Chief Librarian at Paul, Weiss, Rifkind, Wharton & Garrison, 1285 Avenue of the Americas, New York, NY 10019.

Storage Library	3,700	1,500
Total	18,850	17,275

Our space needs for staff and collections were based on a five-year growth projection. Planning for the new library began as far back as November 1982 when we began to project staff and collection space and the role technology would play in the function and design of the facility. Although the library's first meeting with the architects was in January 1983, there was little interaction between us again until March 1985, when we began to meet regularly to formulate floor plans. For the next nine months, many floor plans were considered, and modifications and changes were made often, since ultimately the library design required the approval of the firm's administrators, several lawyers, committees, and the architects. At last construction began in November 1985 and continued for nearly a year thereafter (see Figure D.1).

The firm moved to its present location in September 1986, consolidating its four New York offices (and three libraries) into one. The library staff moved in two weeks before the rest of the firm. Our move began on a Wednesday night and was complete by midday Monday. During the move, and until the rest of the firm joined us two weeks later, we continued to provide reference and research to our lawyers. Surrounded by construction work in progress, we hired extra messengers to carry materials back and forth between the old and new offices.

During the design phase, we encountered a number of problems. First, because the space available for the Main Library staff and collections was not large enough, we had to decide who and what would be located one floor above. By installing a dumbwaiter to transport books between the two floors, we were able to move Technical Services upstairs with minimal disruption in operations. One advantage of this plan was that the staff was given external window space.

Even after the decision was made to move Technical Services upstairs, we were still lacking the space we wanted for reference librarians, offices and interlibrary loan. We felt very strongly that these offices should be close to the book collection and the reference desk. It seemed an impossible situation until the architect sug-

FIGURE D.1.

gested that we move the ladies' room to the other side of the floor and locate the staff offices where the ladies' room had been. Despite the high cost, it was decided that this was the most efficient and economical use of space in the long run (see Figure D.2).

Another problem could have been the structural support columns, which appear at regular intervals throughout the library. The design firm creatively spaced the lateral compact shelving at each column, a solution that allowed us to maintain uniform aisle widths and still use space efficiently to provide the programmed linear feet of shelving.

TABLE D.1. Library Statistics (1987)

Useable area	17,275 sq. ft.
Staff size	
Professional	11
Support	25
Seating for users	75
Population served	335 lawyers, 70 paralegals
Collection size	75,000 volumes (including microforms)
Date of completion	September 1986

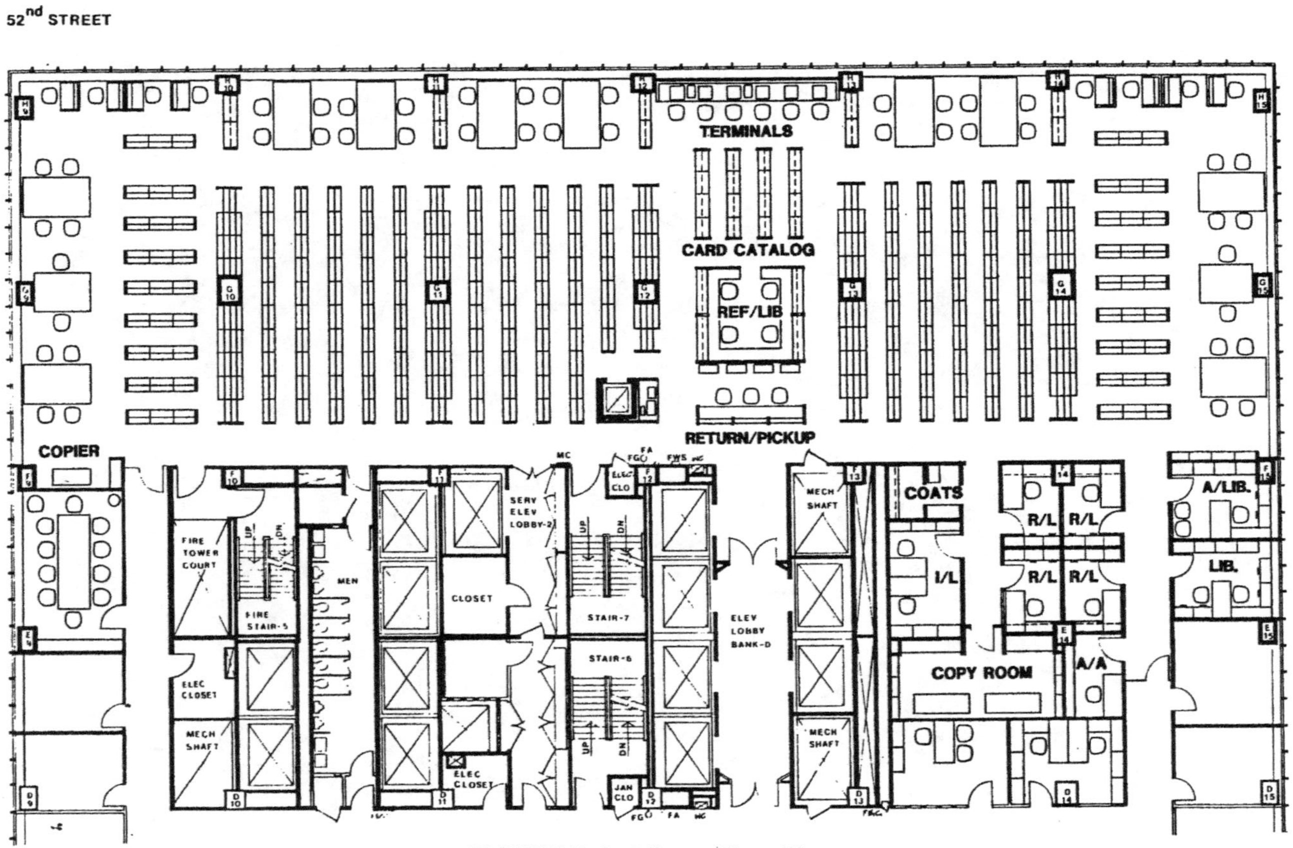

FIGURE D.2. Library Floor Plan

Index

Air conditioning 113-114
  bibliography on 143-144
Aisles, design of 94-95,96
Architects, role of 56-58,67-79
Automation, bibliography on 144-145

Bibliography on library planning 133-157
Budgets, role of 77-78
Building construction coordinators, role of 62

Carpeting 115
Carrels 118-119
Case studies, bibliography on 153-156
Ceilings, walls, and floors 114-115
Chairs, selection of 30-32
Collections, estimation of size of 82
  planning for growth of 101
Collegiate sci-tech library facilities,
    planning for 179-187
Compact shelving 92-94
Computer rooms, design of 123-124
Computer-aided design and drafting 73-74, 106
Computers, impact of on designing 100-101
Conceptual design, nature of 71-73
Conference exhibits of new equipment 45
Conference rooms 119
Construction administration 76-77
Construction features, statement of in
    program 10
Consultants, role of 56
Containers for moving 35-36
Contract documents 76
Convenience, relation to floor plans 21-22
Cooperative efforts in library planning 53-65
Cost factors, relation to floor planning 22-23
Creativity, role of 4-5
  in furnishing libraries 111-112

Deliverables, summary of 78-79
Delivery of equipment 33
Design development, nature of 74-76
Drawing floor plans 25-26

Electronic equipment, selection of 121-123
Electronic workstations 121-123
Engineering staff, role of in planning 63
Environmental aspects 20-22,112-113
Equipment, selection of 32-33
Equipment space, furnishing of 121-123
Esthetic factors, relation to floor plans 23-24

Facilities planning departments, role of 64
Facsimile, bibliography on 150-151
Field representatives, role of 58-59
Floor plans, bibliography on 140-141
  drawing of 25-26
  factors affecting 15-25
Floors 114-115
Four-post shelving 86-87
Furniture, in public user space 118-120
  selection of 30-32,117-118
Furniture suppliers, bibliography on 146-147

Gathering information in pre-planning stages 42-45

Heating 113-114
  bibliography on 143-144

Indexing services, areas for 119-120
Installation schedules for equipment 33
Interior design, bibliography on 140-141
Interior designers, role of 64,99-109

Law library facilities, plans for 189-193
Libraries, differences among types of 6-8
Library automation, effect on designs 123-124

195

Library planners. *See* Planners
Library planning, overview of 3-8
Library programs 67,69-71
　preparation of 9-14
Library staff, role of in planning 61
Library users, nature of 10
Lighting 116-117
　bibliography on 141-143
　planning for 102

Maintenance contracts for equipment 33
Metal shelving, selection of 83-87
　thickness of 86
Microform equipment, bibliography on 148-149
Microform storage units 18-19
Moving companies, selection of 35-36
Moving libraries 35-40
　preparation for 36-40
　scheduling of 38

Noise, relation to floor plans 20-21

Offices, furnishing of 126-128
Online user education 124-126
Open-landscape offices 126-127
Oregon Regional Primate Research Center, planning for 159-164

Paul, Weiss, Rifkind, Wharton & Garrison Library 189-193
Performance of equipment 32-33
Periodicals, shelving for 88,89
Pharmaceutical library facilities, planning for 165-178
Photocopy equipment, bibliography on 149-150
Planners, role of 53-55
Planning, bibliography on 133-157
Planning committees, role of 55
Planning facilities, stages of 5-6
Planning team, bibliography on 138-139
Planning team
　make-up of 12-14
Posts and shafts, effect of on shelving areas 95,97-98

Pre-planning 41-52
　bibliography on 136-137
Product reliability of equipment 32-33
Programs. *See* Library programs
Punch lists 109

Qualitative design issues 103
Quantitative design issues 100

Raceways 120
Reference materials, shelving for 88-91
Research library facilities, planning for 159-164
Rolling shelving 92-94

Safety factors, relation to floor plans 24-25
Schematic design, nature of 73-74
Security, bibliography on 151-152
Seminars on library moving 44-45
Services offered by libraries, statement of in program 11-12
Shafts and posts, effect of on designs 95-97,98
Shelving, bibliography on 148
　capacity of 17-18
　compact 92-94
　estimation of needs for 81-82
　metal 83-87
　for periodicals 88
　for reference materials 88-91
　selection of 81-98
　wood 87-88
Signage 105
Space requirements 15-20
　statement of in program 11
Space utilization 15-27
Spacing for furniture 19
Specialized work stations 104
Staff/user interaction 103
Standards for space planning 70
Statistics, gathering of 12
Supervision of library moves 38-39
Suppliers of library equipment, bibliography on 146-150
Swarthmore College's Science and Engineering Library 179-187

Index

Tables, selection of 30-31
Telecommunication staff, role of in planning 63
Telecommunications, bibliography on 150-151
Three-dimensional drawings 106,108
Traffic, relation to floor plans 21
Two-dimensional drawings 106,107
Two-post shelving 83-84,86

Upjohn Company Corporate Technical Library, planning for 165-178
User space, enhancement of 105-106
Users, role of in planning 59-60

Ventilating 113-114
  bibliography on 143-144
Vertical files 18
Visiting other libraries 45-51

Walls 114-115
Weeding collections 36-37
White noise 126
Wiring 115-116
  of work stations 120
Wish lists 77-78
Wood shelving, selection of 87-88
Work areas, sizes of 19-20
Work stations, specialized 104

For Product Safety Concerns and Information please contact our EU representative GPSR@taylorandfrancis.com
Taylor & Francis Verlag GmbH, Kaufingerstraße 24, 80331 München, Germany

www.ingramcontent.com/pod-product-compliance
Lightning Source LLC
Chambersburg PA
CBHW052117300426
44116CB00010B/1706